The Think-Aloud Contro

in   ırcn

The Think-Aloud Controversy in Second Language Research aims to answer key questions about the validity and uses of think-alouds, which are verbal reports completed by research participants while they perform a task. It offers an overview of how think-alouds have been used in language research and presents a quantitative meta-analysis of findings from studies involving verbal tasks and think-alouds. The book begins by presenting the theoretical background and empirical research that has examined the reactivity of think-alouds, then offers guidance regarding the practical issues of data collection and analysis, and concludes by providing implications for the use of think-alouds in language research. With its focus on a much-discussed and somewhat controversial data elicitation method in language research, this timely work is relevant to students and researchers from all theoretical perspectives who collect first or second language data. It serves as a valuable guide for any language researcher who is considering using think-alouds.

Melissa A. Bowles is Assistant Professor of Spanish, Linguistics, and SLATE (Second Language Acquisition and Teacher Education) at the University of Illinois at Urbana-Champaign. Her main research interests are instructed second/heritage language acquisition and research methods.

Second Language Acquisition Research Series:
Theoretical and Methodological Issues
Susan M. Gass and Alison Mackey, Editors

Monographs on Theoretical Issues:
Schachter/Gass Second Language Classroom Research: Issues and
Opportunities (1996)
Birdsong Second Language Acquisition and the Critical Period
Hypotheses (1999)
Ohta Second Language Acquisition Processes in the Classroom:
Learning Japanese (2001)
Major Foreign Accent: Ontogeny and Phylogeny of Second
Language Phonology (2001)
VanPatten Processing Instruction: Theory, Research, and
Commentary (2003)
VanPatten/Williams/Rott/Overstreet Form-Meaning Connections
in Second Language Acquisition (2004)
Bardovi-Harlig/Hartford Interlanguage Pragmatics: Exploring
Institutional Talk (2005)
Dörnyei The Psychology of the Language Learner: Individual
Differences in Second Language Acquisition (2005)
Long Problems in SLA (2007)
VanPatten/Williams Theories in Second Language Acquisition
(2007)
Ortega/Byrnes The Longitudinal Study of Advanced L2 Capacities
(2008)
Liceras/Zobl/Goodluck The Role of Formal Features in Second
Language Acquisition (2008)

Monographs on Research Methodology:
Tarone/Gass/Cohen Research Methodology in Second Language
Acquisition (1994)
Yule Referential Communication Tasks (1997)
Gass/Mackey Stimulated Recall Methodology in Second Language
Research (2000)

Markee Conversation Analysis (2000)

Gass/Mackey Data Elicitation for Second and Foreign Language Research (2007)

Duff Case Study Research in Applied Linguistics (2007)

McDonough/Trofimovich Using Priming Methods in Second Language Research (2008)

Larson-Hall A Guide to Doing Statistics in Second Language Research Using SPSS (2009)

Dörnyei /Taguchi Questionnaires in Second Language Research: Construction, Administration, and Processing, Second Edition (2009)

Bowles The Think-Aloud Controversy in Second Language Research (2010)

Of Related Interest:

Gass Input, Interaction, and the Second Language Learner (1997)

Gass/Sorace/Selinker Second Language Learning Data Analysis, Second Edition (1998)

Mackey/Gass Second Language Research: Methodology and Design (2005)

Gass/Selinker Second Language Acquisition: An Introductory Course, Third Edition (2008)

The Think-Aloud Controversy in Second Language Research

Melissa A. Bowles

Routledge
Taylor & Francis Group

NEW YORK AND LONDON

First published 2010
by Routledge
270 Madison Avenue, New York, NY 10016

Simultaneously published in the UK
by Routledge
2 Park Square, Milton Park, Abingdon, Oxon OX14 4RN

*Routledge is an imprint of the Taylor & Francis Group, an
informa business*

© 2010 Taylor & Francis

Typeset in Sabon by Swales & Willis Ltd, Exeter, Devon
Printed and bound in the United States of America
on acid-free paper by Walsworth Publishing Company, Marceline, MO

Library of Congress Cataloging-in-Publication Data
Bowles, Melissa A.
  The think-aloud controversy in second language research /
  Melissa A. Bowles.
  p. cm. — (Second language acquisition research series: theoretical and methodological issues)
  Includes bibliographical references.
  [etc.]
  1. Second language acquisition—Research. 2. Language and languages—
Research. 3. Thought and thinking—Study and teaching.
  4. English language—Study and teaching—Foreign speakers. I. Title.
  P118.2.B69 2010
  418.007'2—dc22
  2009045982

ISBN13: 978–0–415–99483–5 (hbk)
ISBN13: 978–0–415–99484–2 (pbk)
ISBN13: 978–0–203–85633–8 (ebk)

Contents

Acknowledgments   xi

Introduction   1

1   The Use of Verbal Reports in Language Research   5

History of Data Collection with Verbal Reports 5
In Non-SLA Fields 5
In L1 and L2 Research 6
L1 Research 6
Reading 6
Writing 6
Language Testing 7
L2 Research 7
Reading 8
Writing 9
Translation 9
Interlanguage Pragmatics 9
Conversational Interaction Research 10
Attention and Awareness 11
Implicit and Explicit L2 Knowledge 12

2   Controversy Over the Use of Think-Alouds: Reactivity   13

Classifying Verbal Reports: Ericsson and Simon's Model 13
Challenges to the Validity of Verbal Reports:
Veridicality and Reactivity 13
Main Predictions of Ericsson and Simon's Model 14
Responding to Challenges: Investigations of Validity
in Cognitive Psychology 15
Studies Comparing Non-Metacognitive Protocols
and Silent Controls 15
Reactivity for Latency but not Accuracy 16

Reactivity for Both Accuracy and Latency 19
Reactivity for Neither Accuracy Nor Latency 21
Studies Investigating the Reactivity of
  Metacognitive Protocols 24
Studies Comparing Metacognitive Protocols
  and Silent Controls 25
  Reactivity for Both Accuracy and Latency 25
    Improved Task Performance 25
    Hindered Task Performance 29
  Reactivity for Accuracy but not for Latency 29
    Improved Task Performace 29
    Hindered Task Performance 36
  Outliers 37
  Reactivity for Latency but not for Accuracy 39
  Reactivity for Neither Latency nor Accuracy 43
Studies Comparing Metacognitive and Non-
  Metacognitive Protocols 46
  Reactivity for Accuracy 46
    Improved Task Performance 46
    Hindered Task Performance 50
  Non-Reactivity for Accuracy 52
  Mixed Results for Reactivity 54
Conclusions 56
  Synthesis: What Makes a Task Amenable to
    Thinking Aloud 59
    Same Task, Same Results 59
    Same Task, Different Results 61
    Similar Tasks, Different Results 62
    Different Tasks, Different Results 63
  Summary 64

3   **Features that Make a Task Amenable to Think-Aloud:**
    A Meta-Analysis of Studies Investigating the Validity
    of Think-Alouds on Verbal Tasks   67

Reactivity Studies in SLA 67
  Leow and Morgan-Short (2004) 67
  Bowles and Leow (2005) 67
  Sachs and Polio (2007) 68
  Sachs and Suh (2007) 69
  Rossomondo (2007) 70
  Bowles (2008) 70
  Yoshida (2008) 71
  Sanz et al. (2009) 72

Polio and Wang (in review) 73
Synthesizing Research on Reactivity 76
Meta-Analysis 78
   Identification of Studies 79
      Selection Criteria 80
         Inclusion Criteria 80
         Exclusion Criteria 81
      Coding 81
      Calculation of Effect Sizes 82
      Combining Effect Sizes 83
      Analysis of the Homogeneity of Effect Sizes 84
Results 86
   Publication Characteristics 86
   Learner Characteristics 87
   Effects of Type of Report on Post-Test Performance 90
      Effect of Type of Report on Text
         Comprehension 93
      Effect of Type of Report on Receptive
         Form Learning 94
      Effect of Type of Report on Productive
         Form Learning 95
      Effect of Type of Report on Latency 96
   Effects of Language of Report on Post-Test
      Performance 96
      Effects of Language of Report on Text
         Comprehension 96
      Effects of Language of Report on Receptive
         Form Learning 97
      Effects of Language of Report on Productive
         Form Learning 98
      Effects of Language of Report on Latency 98
   Effects of Language of Task on Post-Test
      Performance 99
      Effects of Language of Task on Text
         Comprehension 99
      Effects of Language of Task on Receptive
         Form Learning 99
      Effects of Language of Task on Productive
         Form Learning 100
      Effects of Language of Task on Latency 101
   Effects of Type of Task on Post-Test Performance 102
      Effects of Type of Task on Text
         Comprehension 102

Effects of Type of Task on Receptive
Form Learning 103
Effects of Type of Task on Productive
Form Learning 104
Effects of Type of Task on Latency 105
Effects of L2 Proficiency on Post-Test Performance 105
Discussion 106
Summary of Major Findings 110
Areas in Need of Future Research 110

4   **Data Collection Considerations**   113

Instructions for Research Participants 113
Informed Consent 113
Think-Aloud Instructions 114
Re-iterate the Reason for Thinking Aloud 114
Provide Instructions about How to
Think-Aloud 115
Warm-Up Task 117
Type of Language Task 117
Type and Language of Verbalization 118
Timing and Think-Alouds 119
Recording Think-Alouds 120
Ensuring Validity 120

5   **Data Analysis Considerations**   123

Transcription 123
Ensuring Representativeness 125
Coding 126
Coding Example 1: Rosa and O'Neill (1999) 126
Coding Example 2: Seng and Hashim (2006) 128
Coding Example 3: Woodfield (2008) 130
Inter-Coder Reliability 136

6   **Conclusion** 137

Future Research Directions 138

Appendix A: Studies Included in the Meta-Analysis   141
Appendix B: Summary of Unique Sample Studies   143
Notes   149
References   151
Index   167

Acknowledgments

There are many people without whom this manuscript would not have been possible. First and foremost, I would like to thank Sue Gass and Alison Mackey, the editors of the Second Language Acquisition Research series, for including my book among their volumes. My contacts at Routledge, Ivy Ip and Mike Andrews, were incredibly helpful throughout the manuscript review and submission process.

I also owe a debt of gratitude to the faculty at Georgetown University who inspired me to use think-alouds in my research (as well as to question their use and validity). Ron Leow, Cristina Sanz, and RuSan Chen, my dissertation committee members, you have seen just how far this project has come.

I would also like to express my gratitude to the following friends and colleagues who have provided comments and suggestions on earlier versions of this manuscript, or parts thereof: Silvina Montrul, Charlene Polio, Rebecca Sachs, and Wataru Suzuki.

And most of all, I thank Charles, Jake, and Blue for putting up with me while I spent long hours working on this manuscript. Without your love, support, and encouragement, this would have been impossible.

Introduction

Language acquisition research involves measuring and describing learners' knowledge of a language. But a perennial problem is that the evidence stemming from learners' language production is incomplete; some other method is needed to elicit a more complete data set. Verbal reports have been used extensively in first (L1) and second (L2) language research to provide insight on a variety of issues that production data alone cannot address, such as language learners' cognitive processing, thought processes, and strategies. Simply put, verbal reports are a learner's comments recorded either while s/he completes a task or sometime thereafter. Verbal reports completed during a task are referred to as concurrent reports (or think-alouds) and those completed after the task are referred to as retrospective reports.

This book seeks to provide some answers to questions about the validity and use of think-alouds, serving as a guide for any language researcher who is considering using them as a research tool. Its focus is on the unique validity concerns, data collection methods, and research questions associated with think-alouds. Readers interested in the use of retrospective reports, particularly as they have been used in second language acquisition (SLA) research, are referred to Gass and Mackey (2000), which is indispensable on the topic of stimulated recalls. Stimulated recalls are a subset of retrospective reports that occur after task completion but include a video- or audio-recording to serve as a stimulus for the participant.

In addition to being used in fields as diverse as accounting, economics, and market research, verbal reports are used by language researchers from a variety of theoretical perspectives, including conversational analytic (CA) (Walters, 2007), sociocultural (Poehner, 2007; Smagorinsky, 2001; Swain, 2006a, 2006b), and cognitivist perspectives (Leow, 1997a, 2001a; Qi & Lapkin, 2001; Rosa & Leow, 2004a; Rosa & O'Neill, 1999; Sachs & Polio, 2007). The starting assumptions about verbal reports vary, however, based on theoretical position.

The foundations for CA and sociocultural theory come from the work of sociocultural psychologist Lev Vygotsky. Through his work with children, Vygotsky developed a series of hypotheses about the role of language in human development. Vygotsky claimed that at the earliest stages of development, a child's speech is entirely social. As the child grows and develops, speech branches out to have not only a social function – to communicate with others – but also a separate, private function, for the self. This type of speech (referred to as egocentric speech) is inner speech that helps humans to regulate their own behavior and cognitive processes. Vygotsky claimed that in cognitively complex or demanding situations, inner speech could be used, either as subvocalizations, or as audible speech.

Furthermore, private speech continues to be accessible throughout a human's lifetime. Through verbalization, new knowledge and insights may be gained, and control over planning, attending, and remembering can be achieved. In other words, the opportunity to talk about instructional materials mediates the internalization of knowledge (Vygotsky, 1987, p. 86). For this reason, CA and sociocultural theorists view learning as something that *emerges* through verbalization. Recent SLA literature has reflected this view that verbal reports, through collaborative dialogue or "languaging" (Swain, 2006a, 2006b) can be a tool for learning, since the very act of verbalizing is believed to alter thought processes.

In contrast, cognitivist SLA researchers are interested in being able to use verbalizations as a window into the minds of learners, as a means of capturing their internal thought processes. Crucially, an underlying assumption for cognitivists is that verbalizations can accurately reflect thought processes (rather than alter them) and can therefore be a data collection tool. In this regard, cognitivist SLA researchers take the position that psychologists Ericsson and Simon (1984, 1993) espouse, that one purpose of using verbal reports is to gain insight into learners' cognitive processes. From both perspectives, then, it is critical to determine whether (or to what extent) verbalizing while completing a language task actually reflects (or alters) natural thought processes.

For years, despite some concerns over their validity (e.g. Ellis, 2001; Jourdenais, 2001), cognitivists tacitly assumed that verbal reports provided an accurate reflection of learners' thought processes, or that they did *not* change thought processes substantially. Since Leow and Morgan-Short's (2004) study, which was the first in SLA to compare the performance of participants in silent and think-aloud conditions, awareness about the issue has been raised.

This book is intended as a resource for language researchers from any perspective who are considering using think-alouds. In the following six chapters, the book provides an overview of how think-alouds have been used in language research and presents a meta-analysis of findings from reactivity studies involving verbal tasks that compared +/– think-aloud conditions. It therefore provides evidence about the conditions under which think-alouds are likely to accurately reflect thought processes as well as about the circumstances under which they are likely to alter thought processes, either impeding learning or serving as a source of learning. The goals of the book are twofold – to clear up some of the controversy surrounding the use of think-alouds, on the one hand, and to provide concrete recommendations for their implementation as a research tool, on the other.

Chapter 1 places think-alouds within their historical context, tracing the evolution of verbal reports as they have been used in cognitive psychology starting in the 1930s and 1940s and continuing until the present day. In addition, the chapter discusses the ways verbal reports have been used in both first and second language research since the 1970s. Examples from a wide array of theoretical perspectives and areas of research are represented to demonstrate the variety of research questions that think-alouds have been used to answer. Among the areas discussed are reading, writing, strategy use, translation, conversational interaction, interlanguage pragmatics, and language testing.

Chapter 2 categorizes verbal reports according to the well-known model from cognitive psychologists Ericsson and Simon (1984, 1993) and sets out the basic predictions of the model. It then presents critiques of verbal reports from both cognitive psychology (where the method has been used systematically since the 1950s to collect introspective data) and language research (where the method has been used more recently). Critics have alleged that requiring participants to think aloud while they perform a task may affect the task performance and therefore not be a true reflection of normal cognitive processing. The chapter concludes by presenting data from dozens of studies that have compared the performance of participants who verbalized and those who did not, involving both problem-solving (non-verbal) and language-related (verbal) tasks.

Chapter 3 concludes the theoretical section of the book, describing the selection and coding of studies included in a meta-analysis on the validity of think-alouds. Results of the meta-analysis are used to provide insight into the conditions under which think-alouds are (and are not) reactive, and to provide direction for future research.

Chapters 4 and 5 focus on the more pragmatic issues of how to collect and analyze think-aloud data. The information is intended to serve as a guide for researchers planning to use the think-aloud method in their studies. So that readers can apply the guidance to their own research questions and settings, the chapters contain examples and excerpts of actual think-aloud data from published research with a variety of language tasks. The information is designed to be specific to the needs of language researchers, but at the same time broadly applicable to the many different types of research in the field.

Chapter 6 is the conclusion, which summarizes the overall findings with regard to think-alouds and proposes implications and future research directions.

1 The Use of Verbal Reports in Language Research

History of Data Collection with Verbal Reports

In Non-SLA Fields

Verbal reports have been used as a data collection tool in psychology since the early twentieth century. The earliest studies in this vein (e.g. Ewert & Lambert, 1932; Katona, 1940) investigated the effects of experimenter-provided verbalizations on participants' task perform-ance. In these studies, the experimenter would first identify a series of principles necessary for successful completion of the problem-solving task and would then state those essential principles to one group of participants, hypothesizing that this verbalization would improve participants' performance as compared to a control group of partic-ipants who did not receive any such verbal guidance. By the 1950s, in large part as a result of the ideological shift away from behavior-ism, psychologists began re-directing the focus of experimentation to participants' own cognitive processes. It was at this point that researchers began to investigate the effects of participants' own ver-balizations on task performance (e.g. Brunk et al., 1958; Gagné & Smith, 1962; Hafner, 1957; Marks, 1951).

In the intervening decades, there has been a marked increase in the use of verbal reports to study cognitive processes, so much so that "both concurrent and retrospective verbal reports are now generally recognized as major sources of data on subjects' cognitive processes in specific tasks" (Ericsson & Simon, 1993, p. xi). The collection of verbal reports has become standard in many fields, ranging from accounting (e.g. M. Anderson, 1985), anthropology (e.g. Clark, 1987), care planning (e.g. Fowler, 1997), counseling (e.g. Bozarth, 1970), drug and alcohol addiction treatment (e.g. Midanik & Hines, 1991), ergonomics (e.g. Brinkman, 1993), marketing (e.g. Biehal & Chakravarti, 1989), psychology (e.g. K. M. Robinson, 2001), and software engineering (e.g. Hughes & Parkes, 2003), to medicine, where verbal reports are routinely used in the treatment of autism and developmental disorders (e.g. Berg, 2002; Friedman & Mulhern, 1976), as well as in speech pathology (e.g. Karsenty, 2001), neurology (e.g. Chan et al., 2002), cardiology (e.g. Bernardi et al., 2000), and nursing (e.g. Greenwood & King, 1995). In each of these fields, verbal reports are used to provide insight into participants', clients', or patients' decisions, actions, and behaviors.

In L1 and L2 Research

L1 Research

READING

Verbal reports have also been used in L1 research, with the earliest studies investigating L1 reading and writing. A number of studies since the 1980s have used think-alouds to probe students' reading strategies (e.g. A. D. Cohen, 1986; A. D. Cohen, 1987; Earthman, 1992; Farrington-Flint & Wood, 2007; Folger, 2001; Gordon, 1990; Hyona & Nurminen, 2006), and some have used verbalization as a technique to compare the reading strategies of gifted, average, and learning disabled students (e.g. Fehrenbach, 1991; McGuire & Yewchuk, 1996). Others have investigated specific reading strategies common to elementary school children (e.g. Alvermann, 1984), middle school students (e.g. Harmon, 2000), and higher-level readers (e.g. Rosenshine & Meister, 1992). Think-alouds have also been used as a measurement instrument, to assess students' text comprehension while they read (e.g. Nist & Kirby, 1986; Wade, 1990), and as one component of instructional interventions designed to help students improve their reading abilities (Baumann et al., 1993; Robertson, 1995; Walczyk et al., 2001; Wilhelm, 2001).

WRITING

Think-alouds have also been used extensively to investigate L1 writing processes. Studies comparing the cognitive processes involved in writing different kinds of texts (Durst, 1987) and investigating the processes of revision and editing (e.g. Breetvelt, 1994; Zellermayer & Cohen, 1996) are common and have revealed much information not available from the finished product alone. And, as in L1 reading research, teachers have used think-alouds as an instructional technique to help students to view writing as an expression of their inner dialogue (Box, 2002; Cushman, 2002; Fresch et al., 1998; Scardamalia, 1984).

In recent years, verbal reports have also had a place in language testing. (Green (1998) provides an excellent book-length treatment of how verbal report methodology has been applied in language testing.) In brief, though, think-alouds have been used for predominantly two purposes – to gather validity evidence for language tests and to examine test-taking strategies. Specifically, recent studies have used think-alouds to examine the construct validity of reading comprehension tests (e.g. N. J. Anderson et al., 1991; Wijgh, 1996), as well as to investigate the comparative validity of multiple-choice, short-answer, and cloze items (e.g. Storey, 1997; H. Wang, 2001). A number of studies conducted on test-taking strategies have asked students to think aloud as they read and answer test items in their L1, in lieu of the more traditional approach of asking students explicitly what strategies they use (Gavin, 1989; S. P. Norris, 1990).

L2 Research

Introspective methods, including verbal reports, have also been used extensively as a data elicitation technique in second/foreign language research. Since SLA was first studied systematically in the early 1970s, there has been some debate over the use of the data, with researchers like Selinker (1972) indicating that researchers should "focus analytical attention" only on observable data, "the utterances which are produced when a learner attempts to say sentences of a TL [target language]" (pp. 213–214). That is, in Selinker's view, only learners' production data should be used in formulating theories and conducting research about SLA. However, others, such as Corder (1973), disagreed with this view, arguing that production data from language learners provide only a small piece of the language learning puzzle. Many processes in language learning are not directly observable, and cannot be understood just on the basis of what a learner says in the target language. As Corder pointed out, in order to understand how language learning works, it is also necessary to determine what learners think *about* their own production. Corder believed that this type of information could only be gathered through introspective methods.

While the debate over the use of verbal reports continues today, many researchers in the field have used verbal reports, both concurrent and retrospective, and have argued that they have been able to find out more than they would have otherwise known without such introspective measures. In the field of L2 research, it is often difficult to determine the reasoning behind learners' target language use. Without the assistance of verbal reports and other introspective measures, such reasoning is often inferred from the learners' language use (and from the mistakes they make in language production). However, inferring why learners make certain errors in the target language or why they produce language in the way they do can be risky. As Gass and Mackey (2000) point out, "understanding the source of second language production is problematic because often there are multiple explanations for production phenomena that can only be assessed by exploring the process phenomena" (p. 26). If researchers simply infer what learners are thinking based on their production data, they risk missing at least part of what is really going on as learners process and produce a second language. Verbal reports therefore enable researchers to gain access to cognitive processes that are often unavailable by other means.

Because verbal reports have the advantage of providing insight into learners' cognitive processes, they have been used in a number of areas of L2 research, including L2 reading and writing (e.g. Cavalcanti & Cohen, 1990; A. D. Cohen, 1987; A. D. Cohen & Cavalcanti, 1987; Hosenfeld, 1976, 1977, 1979, 1984), comparisons between L1 and L2 strategies (e.g. Chamot & El Dinary, 1999; J. Davis & Bistodeau, 1993; Nevo, 1989; Yamashita, 2002), L2 test-taking strategies (e.g. A. D. Cohen, 2000; S. P. Norris, 1992; Warren, 1996), translation (e.g. Enkvist, 1995; Færch & Kasper, 1986; Jaaskelainen, 2000; Kern, 1994), interlanguage pragmatics (e.g. A. D. Cohen & Hosenfeld, 1981; Kasper & Blum-Kulka, 1993), and oral interaction research (e.g. Mackey et al., 2000; Nabei & Swain, 2002; Philp, 2003), and L2 attention and awareness studies (e.g. Leow, 1997b, 1998a, 1998b, 1999, 2000, 2001a, 2001b; Rosa & O'Neill, 1999). A brief summary of the kinds of research being carried out with verbal reports in each of these areas follows.

READING

Verbal reports have been used extensively to gain insight into the cognitive processes and strategies learners use while reading in their L2 (e.g. Abbott, 2006; Carrell, 1989; A. D. Cohen, 1986; Lomicka, 1998; Nassaji, 2006; Pressley & Afflerbach, 1995; Pritchard, 1990; Yang, 2006). A number of studies has been conducted on the use of mental translation as a strategy during L2 reading (e.g. Kern, 1994).

The method has also been extended to compare and contrast L1 and L2 reading strategies (e.g. Chamot & El Dinary, 1999; J. Davis & Bistodeau, 1993; Maeng, 2005; Nevo, 1989; Yamashita, 2002) and lexical organization (e.g. Herwig, 2003), as well as to examine the role of the L1 in L2 reading comprehension (Seng & Hashim, 2006) and to investigate the effects of pedagogical techniques such as glossing on L2 readers' text comprehension and vocabulary retention (Bowles, 2004; Ko, 2005; Rott, 2005). Recently, verbal reports have also been used to investigate the reading strategies non-native English-speaking students use when taking standardized English language tests, such as the test of English as a foreign language (TOEFL) (A. D. Cohen & Upton, 2007), and to analyze L2 test-taking strategies (A. D. Cohen, 2000; S. P. Norris, 1992).

WRITING

As in L1 research, verbal reports have also been used to examine thought processes and strategies of L2 writers. Recently, a number of studies has compared L1 and L2 writing strategies (e.g. Beare, 2001; Chenoweth & Hayes, 2001; de Larios et al., 2001; El Mortaji, 2001; Hatasa & Soeda, 2000; Jannausch, 2002; Qi & Lapkin, 2001), while others have investigated the role of the L1 in L2 writing (e.g. C. D. Castro, 2004; D. Castro, 2005; Upton & Lee Thompson, 2001; Uzawa, 1996; W. Wang & Wen, 2002). Think-alouds have also been used in at least one study (Sachs & Polio, 2007) to determine how L2 writers use feedback they receive on compositions.

TRANSLATION

Verbal reports have also been used as a data elicitation technique to examine translation processes. Think-aloud protocols have frequently been used to investigate the processes professional translators use when translating a text from one language to another (e.g. Enkvist, 1995; Færch & Kasper, 1986; Fraser, 1993; Jaaskelainen, 2000; Kern, 1994; Ronowicz et al., 2005; Seguinot, 1996). And, in a slightly different vein, researchers have also employed introspective methodologies, including think-alouds, to study the cognitive processes involved in simultaneous interpreting from one language to another (e.g. Shlesinger, 2000).

INTERLANGUAGE PRAGMATICS

Verbal reports have also been used to gather information about L2 learners' pragmatic competence (A. D. Cohen, 1998a, 1998b; A. D.

Cohen & Hosenfeld, 1981; A. D. Cohen & Olshtain, 1993; Félix-Brasdefer, 2004, 2008; Kasper, 1999; Kasper & Blum-Kulka, 1993; Kasper & Rose, 2002; Liu, 2006; Taguchi, 2008). Verbal report data often enable researchers to better understand the factors that L2 learners take into account when performing speech acts in the L2. Such introspective data can identify ways in which L2 learners differ from native speaker pragmatic norms and may therefore serve to inform pedagogical practice. Specifically, studies in interlanguage pragmatics have investigated differential uses of speech acts across languages (e.g. M. Robinson (1991), as well as compensatory communication strategies in different languages (e.g. Poulisse, 1990; Poulisse et al., 1987). Recently, one study has used think-alouds to examine the validity of discourse completion tasks (DCTs), one of the most commonly used measures of L2 pragmatic competence (Woodfield, 2008).

CONVERSATIONAL INTERACTION RESEARCH

In conversational interaction studies, premised on the Interaction Hypothesis (Long, 1996), verbal reports have been used to gain insight into the cognitive processes of language learners as they interact with either native or non-native speakers in the second/foreign language. A particular kind of retrospective report known as a stimulated recall has been used predominately in this strand of research, since it would not be possible to gather concurrent reports while learners complete oral communication activities. In stimulated recall methodology, learners typically complete an oral interaction task in dyads or small groups while being videotaped and/or audiotaped. Then, a short time after completing the task, the learners view the videotape or listen to the audiotape of themselves completing the task. They are instructed to think back to the time of the task and to describe what they were thinking at *that* time.

Stimulated recall methodology has been used to tap into learners' (H. Carpenter et al., 2006; Mackey et al., 2000; Nabei & Swain, 2002) and interlocutors' (Polio et al., 2006) perceptions about interactional feedback. Specifically, this line of investigation has been concerned with determining (1) what learners actually think when they receive feedback from interlocutors, (2) whether they accurately perceive the feedback as corrective, and (3) whether they "notice the gap" between their interlanguage forms and the target-like forms provided by their interlocutor. This methodology yields interesting and otherwise difficult to gather data about learners' perceptions, but it is not an online measure (i.e. the data are not gathered as the task is being performed, and are therefore subject to confounds such as memory decay).

Philp (2003) used an alternative retrospective method to gather data about learners' attentional processing during interaction (and specifically, after the provision of recasts and distractors). In her study, Philp used an "immediate recall" data elicitation technique in which she recasted learners' non-target-like utterances and then immediately knocked twice on the table, thus cueing the learners to "repeat the last thing [they] heard" (Philp, 2003, p. 108). Philp operationalized noticing as "the learner's cued, correct recall of a recast immediately following production of the recast" (Philp, 2003, p. 105). Thus, immediate recall, like stimulated recall, is collected retrospectively, not concurrently. However, the immediate recall technique elicits recall immediately after brief trials within one task session, so the delay between task completion and recall is considerably shorter than with stimulated recall, further lessening the risk of memory decay.

ATTENTION AND AWARENESS

In the past decade or so, a strand of research has investigated the role of attention and/or awareness in SLA, and verbal reports have been one of the main methodological tools used to measure learners' awareness of features of L2 input (Leow & Bowles, 2005). Almost all theories of SLA posit some role for attention, but the construct is especially emphasized in cognitivist accounts, where it has been proposed that "attention appears necessary for understanding nearly every aspect of second and foreign language learning" (Schmidt, 2001, p. 6).

The specific details of the main theoretical models of attention in SLA (P. Robinson, 1995, 1996; Schmidt, 1990, 1993, 1994, 1995, 2001; Tomlin & Villa, 1994) are not relevant for the current discussion, although interested readers are encouraged to refer to the original sources for more information about the similarities and differences among the models, or to Leow and Bowles (2005) for a review. The most widely accepted view in SLA, which is derived from Schmidt's noticing hypothesis, is that attention is isomorphic with awareness and that without awareness, input is processed too superficially for learning to occur. According to Schmidt's noticing hypothesis, attention controls access to awareness and is responsible for noticing, which is the necessary and sufficient condition for the conversion of input into intake. Furthermore, Schmidt proposes that, in addition to noticing, there is another higher level of awareness, which he refers to as awareness at the level of understanding.

This level of awareness is marked by the ability to analyze, compare, and test hypotheses, and Schmidt believes that this level of awareness leads to deeper learning marked by restructuring and system learning, whereas awareness at the level of noticing leads just to intake.

A number of studies has used think-alouds to gather data on learners' cognitive processes while they interacted with L2 input. The verbalizations were then used to establish the level of awareness during L2 processing. Support for a relationship between different levels of awareness and L2 development has been found in a number of SLA studies, whereto learners who demonstrated higher levels of awareness, including hypothesis-testing and rule formation, consistently outperformed those who demonstrated lower levels of awareness not marked by such cognitive changes (Bowles, 2003; Leow, 1997a, 2001a, 2001b; Rosa, 1999; Rosa & Leow, 2004a, 2004b; Rosa & O'Neill, 1999; Schmidt, 2001).

IMPLICIT AND EXPLICIT L2 KNOWLEDGE

Think-alouds have also been used recently to address a long-standing debate in SLA about the relationship between explicit and implicit L2 knowledge (Ellis, 2004; Hu, 2002). In a recent article on the definition and measurement of explicit knowledge, Ellis (2004) states that "collecting verbal explanations . . . would appear, on the face of it, to provide the most valid measure of a learner's explicit knowledge" (p. 263). Although it is not yet clear what think-alouds will reveal about the nature of and relationship between implicit and explicit language knowledge, it is clear that there will be a role for them in this line of research.

2 Controversy Over the Use of Think-Alouds

Reactivity

Classifying Verbal Reports: Ericsson and Simon's Model

All verbal reports are not identical; rather, there are important differences among verbal reports based on the conditions under which they are collected. Ericsson and Simon's (1984, 1993) classic work on verbalization proposes a typology to categorize verbal reports based on both the temporal frame in which they are collected and on the level of detail of reporting. As mentioned in the Introduction and in Chapter 1, concurrent reports are those collected as subjects verbalize *while* performing the task in question, whereas retrospective reports are collected when subjects verbalize some time *after* performing the task. However, there are additional dimensions used to categorize verbal reports, beyond those temporal distinctions. In addition to categorizing verbal reports in terms of temporal space, Ericsson and Simon also distinguish between reports that require subjects to verbalize their thoughts per se and those that require subjects to verbalize additional information, such as explanations and justifications. In previous SLA research (Bowles, 2008; Bowles & Leow, 2005), verbalizations of thoughts per se have been referred to as *non-metalinguistic* and those requiring verbalization of explanations and justifications have been referred to as *metalinguistic*. However, since the studies reported in this book contain both verbal and non-verbal tasks, the broader terms *non-metacognitive* and *metacognitive* will be used to describe them.

Challenges to the Validity of Verbal Reports: Veridicality and Reactivity

Despite the frequency with which verbal reports have been used as a methodological tool to gain insight into L2 learners' cognitive processes, systematic research on their validity in SLA is just beginning. This research is clearly warranted, as Ericsson and Simon (1993), among others, have long been aware of the potential threats to the validity of both retrospective and concurrent verbal reports. For retrospective reports, since participants verbalize some time after completing a task, there is a potential for veridicality. In other words, retrospective verbal reports may not accurately reflect participants' thought processes because they simply may not recall what they were thinking as they completed the given task. The reports may be incomplete as a result. However, this threat can be minimized if there is only a short delay between task performance and verbalization. Similarly, if learners are provided with some stimulus, such as a video or audiotape of their performance, as described in Gass and Mackey's (2000) account of stimulated recalls, the possibility of veridicality is also lessened. For concurrent verbal reports, the main threat to validity does not have to do with veridicality, since verbalization and task performance are concomitant. Rather, their validity is questioned because it is not known whether the act of verbalizing while completing a task is reactive, acting as an additional task and altering cognitive processes rather than providing a true reflection of thoughts, as Ellis (2001) and Jourdenais (2001) have suggested in the SLA literature. Since the focus of this book is think-alouds, the issue of reactivity will receive the greatest attention.

Main Predictions of Ericsson and Simon's Model

In addition to categorizing verbal reports, Ericsson and Simon's (1993) model makes predictions about their validity. Specifically, it predicts that verbalization of thoughts per se (which Ericsson and Simon refer to as Type 1 verbalizations, or non-metacognitive verbalizations) will be largely non-reactive; that is, they will reflect the nature of cognitive processes fairly accurately, while slowing processing slightly. Furthermore, the model predicts that verbalization of justifications or additional specific information (Type 2 and 3 verbalizations, or metacognitive verbalizations) may be more reactive, not only slowing processing but also potentially causing changes in cognitive processing.

Despite the frequency with which verbal reports are gathered in language research, their use has been criticized by a number of sources on the grounds that verbalization may alter cognitive processes (e.g. Ellis, 2001; Jourdenais, 2001; Nisbett & Wilson, 1977; Payne et al., 1978). The use of verbal reports has been harshly criticized by some who believe that verbalization of thoughts during language tasks imposes an additional processing load on the subjects, and is therefore not a pure measure of their thoughts. For instance, Jourdenais (2001) cautions that "the think aloud data collection method itself acts as an additional task which must be considered carefully when examining learner performance" (p. 373).

Responding to Challenges: Investigations of Validity in Cognitive Psychology

Although only a handful of studies to date have investigated the reactivity of verbal protocols on verbal tasks, studies examining the effects of verbalization on problem-solving and decision-making tasks have been conducted in the field of cognitive psychology since the 1950s. The findings of those studies, which are presented in the remainder of this chapter, can be used to evaluate the challenges to the validity of think-alouds.

Studies Comparing Non-Metacognitive Protocols and Silent Controls

In their seminal work, Ericsson and Simon (1993) reviewed a number of studies comparing non-metacognitive verbal reports to silent controls. Their synthesis of the results reveals a relatively consistent pattern of findings across studies – that non-metacognitive verbalizations do not influence cognitive processes when compared to silent control groups. This finding of non-reactivity suggests that non-metacognitive verbalization may be a valid method of capturing internal thought processes. However, their findings indicate that, overall, verbalization *does* tend to be reactive for latency (solution time) because the additional time needed for verbalization increases the overall solution time. These findings support the predictions of their model, which claims that verbalization of thoughts per se, without the requirement to verbalize justifications, should provide a fairly pure reflection of thought processes.

A thorough search in the literature revealed ten additional studies not described in Ericsson and Simon (1993) that investigated the reactivity of non-metacognitive verbal reports (M. Anderson, 1985; Biggs et al., 1993; Brinkman, 1993; Deffner, 1989; Knoblich & Rhenius, 1995; Lass et al., 1991; Rhenius & Deffner, 1990; Rhenius & Heydemann, 1984; Stratman & Hamp-Lyons, 1994; Williams & Davids, 1997). These studies are drawn from diverse disciplines and involve a variety of participants and task types. Despite this apparent heterogeneity, these studies show a relatively uniform pattern of results as well, remarkably similar to those predicted by Ericsson and Simon (1993). Of the ten studies, nine (90 per cent) found verbalization to be non-reactive for accuracy and five (50 per cent) found verbalization to be reactive for latency. Only one study (M. Anderson, 1985) found verbalization to be reactive for both accuracy and latency. The ten studies are briefly reviewed below, in order of their findings; first, those that found reactivity for latency but not for accuracy, then those that found reactivity for both accuracy and latency, and finally those that found reactivity for neither accuracy nor latency. (For a concise summary of findings, see Tables 2.1 through 2.3.)

Reactivity for Latency but not Accuracy

Rhenius and Heydemann (1984) examined the effects of non-metacognitive verbalization as compared to a silent control group on a widely used non-verbal test of intelligence and abstract reasoning known as Raven's Standard Progressive Matrices. In each test item, students must identify the missing segment required to complete the pattern, as shown in the practice item in Figure 2.1.

In the study, 19 undergraduates were randomly assigned to either a non-metacognitive verbalization group or to a silent control group. They were then instructed to solve a series of three matrices of varying levels of difficulty, while their eye movements and gaze duration were measured using eye-tracking software. Although it has begun to be used in linguistics research only recently, eye tracking has been

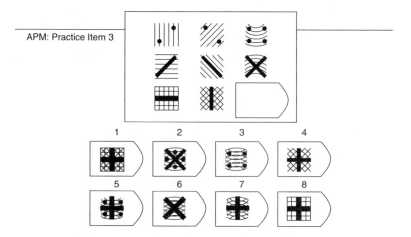

Figure 2.1 Practice Item from Raven's Standard Progressive Matrices

Table 2.1 Studies Comparing Non-Metacognitive Protocols and Silent Controls: Reactivity for Latency but not Accuracy

Study	Participants	Task(s)	Groups	Design	Reactivity	Non-Reactivity
Biggs, Rosman, & Serfenian (1993)	15 equity analysts	Ratio analysis of investment quality of three companies	1. TA (– meta) 2. computer 3. both	Within-subjects	Latency	Accuracy and amount of information
Brinkman (1993)	18 undergraduates	Diagnose problem in 12 faulty networks	1. concurrent TA 2. retrospective TA 3. silent	Within-subjects	Latency	Processing information
Lass, Klettke, Lüer, & Ruhlender (1991)	70 undergraduates	Anagrams	1. TA (– meta) 2. silent	Between-subjects	Latency	Accuracy
Rhenius & Deffner (1990)	1. 24 students 2. 48 students 3. 21 students	1. sentence assembly 2. word and geometrical puzzles 3. Raven's matrices	1. TA (– meta) 2. silent	Between-subjects	Latency[a]	Accuracy
Rhenius & Heydemann (1984)	19 undergraduates	Raven's Matrices	1. control (silent) 2. TA (– meta)	Between-subjects	Latency	Accuracy

Note
– meta = non-metacognitive.
a Differences between solution times of think-aloud and silent groups were significant for all tasks except sentence assembly.

used widely in psychology research on both cognition and the visual system since the 1970s and 1980s.

Participants in the verbalization group were instructed:

> While you solve the problem, please say what comes to mind. Try to think aloud and describe your thinking while you talk. You can decide on your own what you say and how you say it. The important thing is that your speech be as continuous as possible. (Rhenius & Heydemann, 1984, p. 314)

Participants in the control group were not given any additional instructions. Results of *t* tests conducted on mean solution times for the two groups revealed that participants in the verbalization group took significantly longer, on average, to solve the matrices than those in the control group. (For the easiest matrix, average solution time for the silent group was 15.9 seconds, as compared to 48.42 seconds for the verbalization group. Similarly, for the most difficult matrix, average solution time for the silent group was 98.89 seconds, as compared to 131.5 seconds for the verbalization group.) However, there was no statistically significant difference between the two groups in terms of solution accuracy; participants in both groups were able to solve the matrices correctly; those who verbalized simply required more time to arrive at the correct solution than those who were silent.

Rhenius and Deffner (1990), a meta-analysis of three studies comparing non-metacognitive verbalization to silent controls, reveals similar results to those reported in Ericsson and Simon (1993). Using a combined total of 128 undergraduates and four different types of experimental tasks (sentence assembly, word puzzles, geometrical puzzles, and Raven's matrices), Rhenius and Deffner found that think-aloud groups in general required more time to complete tasks than the silent groups. Although details of the statistical analyses are not provided, the authors indicate that in all tasks except sentence assembly, the difference in solution times for think-aloud vs. silent groups was statistically significant. Moreover, the authors report that across the three experiments and the different types of tasks (both verbal and non-verbal) there were no significant differences between think-aloud and silent groups with respect to accuracy.

Lass et al. (1991), in a study similar to that of Rhenius and Heydemann (1984), compared non-metacognitive think-aloud and silent groups in terms of solution time, accuracy, and gaze duration as participants unscrambled anagrams. Seventy undergraduates who participated in the study were randomly assigned to either a verbalization or a control group. Participants in the think-aloud group were instructed: "Say out loud whatever passes through your mind while you are working on the task" (Lass et al., 1991, p. 390). Participants in the control group were simply told to unscramble the anagrams, without any additional instructions. Mean number of errors (incorrect solutions) for each group (think aloud = 4.84, control = 3.72) were submitted to a t test and found to be statistically similar ($t = 1.174$, $df = 62$), indicating that the requirement to verbalize did not affect solution accuracy. However, a t test conducted on the average solution times of the two groups (think aloud = 3029.68 seconds, control = 2395.07 seconds) revealed a statistically significant difference ($t = 2.255$, $df = 62$), indicating that the requirement to verbalize *did* significantly increase solution time.

A study in the field of behavioral decision making (Biggs et al., 1993) used a different population and more complex task type to examine the issue of reactivity, asking 15 equity analysts to provide a ratio analysis of the investment quality of three companies. In the within-subjects design, all of the analysts used computer-based information to rate the three firms on two separate occasions. On one occasion, each analyst completed the ratings silently and on another occasion, each analyst verbalized while completing the ratings. Using each analyst as his/her own control, the authors found that non-metacognitive verbalization did not prove reactive, that is, cause changes in the amount of information searched for, the pattern of acquisition of the information, or the accuracy of the final ratings. However, the task was reactive for latency; analysts took longer to give their ratings when verbalizing than when rating silently.

Another study of reactivity and non-metacognitive verbalization is Brinkman (1993), in ergonomics. In this study, 18 university students were asked to diagnose faults in graphically displayed networks consisting of rows and columns of interconnected logical and gate components for 12 problems. All participants completed the tasks under three conditions: (1) concurrent verbalization, (2) retrospective verbalization, and (3) no verbalization. Results of the within-subjects analysis indicated that concurrent (non-metacognitive) verbalization was not reactive for accuracy (processing of information), although it was reactive for time compared to the no verbalization group.

Reactivity for Both Accuracy and Latency

Only one study reviewed (M. Anderson, 1985) found reactivity for both accuracy and latency. In this accounting study, 15 participants

Table 2.2 Studies Comparing Non-Metacognitive Protocols and Silent Controls: Reactivity for Both Latency and Accuracy

Study	Participants	Task(s)	Groups	Design	Reactivity	Non-Reactivity
M. Anderson (1985)	Five financial analysts, five stockbrokers, and five MBA students	valuation of equity firms	1. TA (– meta) 2. silent	Within-subjects	Latency and accuracy	

Note
– meta = non-metacognitive.

(five financial analysts, five stockbrokers, and five MBA students) were asked to valuate a set of firms that were about to go public in the equity market. The participants were selected to represent differing levels of experience in valuation problems, the financial analysts being the most experienced and the students the least experienced. In a within-subjects randomized block design, each participant valuated 20 firms, verbalizing while valuating half of them. Although the exact verbalization instructions given to participants were not reported in the study, it appears that the verbalizations were non-metacognitive in nature. Results were presented for the three different experience levels. For participants at both ends of the experience scale (the financial analysts and students), verbalization did not have a significant effect on accuracy, although there was a slight decrement in accuracy in the verbalization condition. However, for stockbrokers, who had a medium level of experience with valuation, the requirement to verbalize significantly *improved* accuracy on the valuations. Not surprisingly, participants in all groups took significantly longer to complete the valuations in the verbalization condition than in the silent control condition. The differential findings for reactivity based on valuation experience are important and seem to suggest that verbalization may affect participants differently based on their familiarity or experience with a given task, a result that may have bearing on the use of verbal reports in language research.

Reactivity for Neither Accuracy nor Latency

In a pair of studies, Deffner (1984, 1989) investigated the effects of thinking aloud on various types of non-verbal tasks, such as geometric puzzles and n-term series logic problems. In both studies, a think-aloud group was compared to a silent group, and eye fixations were recorded. In Deffner (1989), 44 undergraduates were randomly assigned to either a think-aloud or a silent condition, and then given a number of logic problems to solve. Deffner found that thinking aloud was not reactive for accuracy, with participants in both groups solving about the same number of logic problems correctly (think aloud = 5.73, silent = 6.36). He also found that the task was not reactive for latency, with the participants in the think-aloud group taking just slightly more time to solve the problems than those in the silent group.

Using a different type of task, a computerized temperature regulation simulation, Knoblich and Rhenius (1995) investigated the effects of non-metacognitive verbalization on solution time,

Table 2.3 Studies Comparing Non-Metacognitive Protocols and Silent Controls: Reactivity for Latency but not Accuracy

Study	Participants	Task(s)	Groups	Design	Reactivity	Non-Reactivity
Deffner (1989)	44 undergraduates	Four and five-term series logic problems	1. silent 2. TA (– meta)	Between-subjects		Accuracy and latency[a]
Knoblich & Rhenius (1995)	37 undergraduates	Computerized temperature regulation simulation (Kühlhaus experiment)	1. silent 2. TA (– meta)	Between-subjects	Eye movement and gaze duration	Accuracy and latency
Stratman & Hamp-Lyons (1994)	12 undergraduates and graduate students	Revision of text	1. TA (– meta) 2. silent	Within- and between-subjects	No statistical analysis[b]	No statistical analysis
Williams & Davids (1997)	20 soccer players	Simulated soccer games	1) TA (– meta) 2) silent	Within-subjects		Accuracy and latency

Notes
– meta = non-metacognitive.
a Participants in the think-aloud group took slightly longer to solve the problems and were marginally less accurate than the participants who did not think aloud. However, neither of these differences was statistically significant.
b Ability to detect and fix organizational errors in the text decreased in the verbalization condition. Detection of pronoun errors and occurrence of word-level errors increased.

accuracy, eye movement, and gaze duration. In the study, 37 undergraduates were randomly assigned to either a think-aloud group or to a silent (control) group to complete a simulation in which they were running a supermarket. During the simulation, the refrigeration system stopped working and their task was to use a lever to regulate the temperature so the remaining food would not spoil. During the experiment, there were 100 opportunities to change the temperature by moving the lever, and a reading was taken by the computer at each interval. These 100 intervals were grouped into four chunks of 25 intervals for purposes of data analysis. A 2×4 analysis of variance (ANOVA) (two groups $\times$ four time intervals) revealed that there was no significant main effect for time $F[1,28] = .57$, $p = .46$, indicating that the task was not reactive for latency. A second 2×4 ANOVA revealed that there was no significant main effect for accuracy of solution $F[1,28] = .47$, $p = .50$, indicating that the task was not reactive for accuracy either. So participants who verbalized while completing the task were equally as accurate and as quick as those who completed the task silently. However, there were significant differences between the think-aloud and control groups in terms of eye movement and gaze duration, suggesting that their processing was in some way affected by the requirement to verbalize, although solution time and accuracy were not compromised.

An experiment in sport and exercise science conducted by Williams and Davids (1997) examined whether concurrent verbalization had an effect on task performance. The participants – 20 soccer players – were divided into two groups based on their amount of experience playing the game. Each participant watched a series of simulated soccer games under two conditions. In one condition participants' eye movements were measured, and in the second condition the participants had to say out loud which part of the screen drew their attention as they watched. While watching the simulation, participants were instructed to indicate where they thought the final pass of the simulation would go. In this study, Williams and Davids reported that there was no difference in performance for either the more or less experienced soccer players across the two conditions and therefore concluded that concurrent verbalization did not result in reactivity for accuracy. Time was held constant for both groups.

Whereas most of the studies reviewed up to this point have used non-verbal tasks, or word-level verbal tasks (such as anagrams), Stratman and Hamp-Lyons (1994) investigated the effects of thinking aloud on an L1 writing task. Twelve graduate and undergraduate university students were instructed to revise two texts. In a within-subjects design, each participant revised one text while thinking aloud and a second text while working silently. Unfortunately, Stratman and Hamp-Lyons were not able to carry out any statistical analyses on the results because of the small sample size. Therefore, the study cannot provide solid evidence about the reactivity of the task. However, looking at trends in the raw data, Stratman and Hamp-Lyons found no difference in participants' ability to detect phrase-level and word-level errors whether they were thinking aloud or revising the text silently. However, the authors suggested that when participants thought aloud, their ability to detect and fix organizational errors in the text decreased and their detection of pronoun errors and the occurrence of word-level errors simultaneously increased.

Studies Investigating the Reactivity of Metacognitive Protocols

A thorough search in the literature revealed 30 empirical studies investigating the reactive effects of metacognitive verbal reports. (For a brief summary of the findings of these studies, see Tables 2.4 through 2.11.) All are from the field of cognitive psychology and make use of problem-solving or decision-making tasks; however, the research designs vary widely.

Twenty-one of the 30 studies (70 per cent) found metacognitive protocols to be reactive for accuracy of task completion, while the remaining nine studies (30 per cent) found metacognitive protocols to be non-reactive for accuracy. Although most of the studies reviewed do not report solution time, ten of the 12 studies that do report some measure of time on task find that metacognitive verbalization significantly affected solution time, thus supporting Ericsson and Simon's prediction that the requirement to verbalize metacognitively (or to provide Type 3 verbalizations) increases solution time (e.g. Ahlum-Heath & di Vesta, 1986; Allwood, 1990; Berardi-Coletta et al., 1995; Brunk et al., 1958; P. A. Carpenter et al., 1990; Fidler, 1983; Gagné & Smith, 1962; Hafner, 1957; K. M. Robinson, 2001; Russo et al., 1989). Only two studies (Schooler et al., 1993; Wilder & Harvey, 1971) report non-reactivity for latency. Because of (1) the heterogeneity of the studies (in terms of task type, experimental condition(s), and participants), and (2) the inconclusive findings overall, each of the studies is reviewed in detail below. First, studies comparing metacognitive reports to silent controls are reviewed, followed by studies comparing metacognitive and non-metacognitive reports to each other. The studies are reviewed in order according to their findings regarding reactivity: first are those that found reactivity for accuracy *and* latency; then those with reactivity for accuracy but not for latency (where time is either not reported or is found not to be statistically different between groups); then those that found reactivity for latency (but not for accuracy); and finally those that found reactivity for neither accuracy nor latency.

Studies Comparing Metacognitive Protocols and Silent Controls

Reactivity for Both Accuracy and Latency

Five of the studies reviewed (Ahlum-Heath & di Vesta, 1986; Brunk et al., 1958; P. A. Carpenter et al., 1990; Gagné & Smith, 1962; Hafner, 1957) found reactivity for both accuracy and time (latency). It appears that these studies fully support Ericsson and Simon's model, which predicts that Type 3 verbalizations, which require additional specific processing, will affect task performance and will, in addition, require extra processing time as compared to other types of verbalizations or to a silent control. Verbalization did not affect task performance in the same way in all studies, however. In three of the five studies (Ahlum-Heath & di Vesta, 1986, Gagné & Smith, 1962; Hafner, 1957) verbalization improved task performance, whereas in the remaining two (Brunk et al., 1958; P. A. Carpenter et al., 1990) it hindered task performance.

IMPROVED TASK PERFORMANCE

Ahlum-Heath and di Vesta (1986) investigated the effects of verbalization on 50 college students' performance on a Tower of Hanoi problem-solving task, while also manipulating the amount of practice. Participants were randomly assigned to one of five groups – (1) verbalization during practice and during task (VP-VC), (2) verbalization during practice and no verbalization during task (VP-NVC), (3) no practice and verbalization during task (NP-VC), (4) no practice and no verbalization during task (NP-NVC), and (5) non-verbal practice and no verbalization during task (NVP-NVC). Participants in the verbalization conditions were required to state, before each move, where each disk was to be moved and why that location was chosen. Results showed that verbalization improved performance (i.e. reduced the number of errors) for participants who had no prior practice with the Tower of Hanoi. No effect for verbalization was found for participants in groups with prior practice. This result may at first seem anomalous, but upon closer examination, it

Table 2.4 Studies Comparing Metacognitive Protocols and Silent Controls: Reactivity for Both Accuracy and Latency

Study	Participants	Task(s)	Groups	Design	Reactivity	Non-Reactivity
Ahlum-Heath & Di Vesta (1986)	50 college students	Tower of Hanoi	1. VP-VC 2. VP-NVC 3. NP-VC 4. NP-NVC 5. NVP-NVC	Between-subjects	Accuracy and latency	
P. A. Carpenter, Just, & Schell (1990)	12 college students	Raven's Progressive Matrices Test	1. silent control 2. concurrent TA + meta	Between-subjects	Accuracy and latency	
Gagné & Smith (1962)	28 ninth- and tenth-grade boys	Tower of Hanoi	1. TA+meta + rule search 2. TA +meta 3. rule search 4. silent control	Between-subjects	Accuracy and latency	
Hafner (1957)	20 fourth-grade children	Stencil Design Test 1 of the Arthur Point Scale of Performance Tests	1. standard admin. (no verbalization) 2. concurrent TA + meta	Between-subjects	Accuracy and latency	

Note
– meta = non-metacognitive.

fits with the predictions of Ericsson and Simon's model. Participants with no practice may have had to expend additional cognitive effort to generate justifications for each move (and therefore the verbalization requirement led them to improved performance). On the other hand, participants who had already practiced the problem type may have begun to justify moves automatically, and verbalizing such reasons likely required no additional processing on their part (and accordingly implied no change in performance). In accordance with the predictions of Ericsson and Simon's (1993) model, an ANOVA also found a significant main effect for time due to verbalization. Participants took longer to solve the problem when they had to verbalize than when they did not. (The Tower of Hanoi is illustrated in Figure 2.2 shown later in the chapter.)

Gagné and Smith (1962) used the Tower of Hanoi problem to investigate the effects of different types of verbalization on performance during a series of training tasks (two-disk to five-disk problems) as well as during transfer to a more complex six-disk problem. Successful completion of the Tower of Hanoi requires participants to move a number of disks from one peg to another, in a specific sequence. Participants were 28 ninth- and tenth-grade boys who had no previous experience with the Tower of Hanoi problem. All participants were introduced to the task and instructed about the rules, after which they were randomly assigned to one of four conditions – (1) group V-SS (verbalizing, solution set), (2) group V (verbalizing, no solution set), (3) group SS (no verbalizing, solution set), or (4) group no (a control group with no verbalizing and no solution set). Group V-SS was instructed to state a reason for each move as they performed the training task and to "think of a general rule by means of which they could tell someone how to solve these problems" (Gagné & Smith, 1962, pp. 13–14). Group V was instructed just to state a reason for each move, without the additional requirement to formulate a rule, whereas group SS was instructed to formulate a rule but not to state a justification for each move. Verbal justifications were all collected concurrently (during the training task) and rules were solicited after task completion. Verbalization was not required on the transfer task, so any effects for the verbalization group on that subsequent task could be attributed to previous verbalization. The researcher noted the number of moves each participant needed to complete each task and also wrote "brief phrase[s] indicating the verbal statement made by each S" (Gagné & Smith, 1962, p. 14). On the training task, results of an ANOVA indicated that between-group differences in number of moves were significant. Post-hoc *t* tests found that the differences were significant at the .01 level for each of the verbalization groups versus each of the non-verbalization groups. Simply stated, "verbalization made a significant difference; solution set instructions made none" (Gagné & Smith, 1962, p. 15). Similarly, results of an ANOVA indicated a significant difference between groups on the transfer task, and post-hoc t tests revealed that (metacognitive) verbalization dramatically improved performance on the transfer task, reducing both the number of moves needed to complete the task and the time taken to find a solution. Participants in the verbalization groups (V and V-SS) required an average of about nine moves to complete the transfer task, as compared to the non-verbalization groups (SS and control), which required an average of about six times as many, or 55 moves! Verbalization correspondingly reduced the amount of time needed to solve the problem, as the verbalization groups solved the problem in an average of about 4 minutes as compared to 10 minutes for the non-verbalization group. The t tests further showed that it was verbalization alone that had a significant effect on performance, as requiring participants to formulate a rule after task completion did not significantly affect performance. These results suggest that the requirement to verbalize caused participants to think more deeply and organize their thoughts differently than the groups not instructed to verbalize. In that way, metacognitive verbalization improved participants' performance on the Tower of Hanoi task.

In Hafner (1957), 20 fourth-grade children were required to complete a series of problem-solving tasks taken from Stencil Design Test 1 of the Arthur Point Scale of Performance Tests. The Stencil Design Test was designed for use with young children and is administered one-on-one. The test administrator begins by presenting each child with 18 cards of different colors. Twelve of the cards have geometrical shapes cut out of them, whereas the remaining six cards have no cut-outs. The child's task is to reproduce designs by placing cut-out cards on top of solid cards of the appropriate color. In the test, each child receives three items that require only two cards and five items that require three cards to produce the design. Children in the control group completed the test silently, according to the standard administration instructions, and those in the experimental (concurrent metacognitive verbalization) group were instructed to "verbalize what they were thinking and doing as they worked" (Hafner, 1957, p. 360). Hafner found that the mean number of correct solutions for the control group was 9.3, as compared to 11.0 for the experimental group, thus indicating that instructions to verbalize improved test performance. His results also indicated that the experimental group required more time to arrive at the solutions.

HINDERED TASK PERFORMANCE

In Brunk et al. (1958), 147 undergraduate students were given an initial Vygotsky-type test (the Ladd test) and then a second, similar test (the PAMS test). All students completed the first test under normal administration conditions, but for the second test students were randomly assigned to either a control (non-metacognitive verbalization) or to a concurrent metacognitive condition. In the metacognitive condition, participants were "requested to tell why [they] placed each block where [they] did and were encouraged to verbalize freely" (Brunk et al., 1958, p. 238). The correlation between scores on the first and second tests was significantly lower under the concurrent metacognitive think-aloud condition than under the non-metacognitive condition. Therefore, the results suggest that requiring the participants to verbalize justifications as they complete the second problem hinders their performance. Also, participants in the justification condition took longer to solve the problems than participants not required to provide such reasoning.

Carpenter et al. (1990) compared the performance of a conventional (silent) control group to a metacognitive think-aloud group on the Raven's Progressive Matrices Test. The 12 college student participants were randomly assigned to one of the groups, and those in the metacognitive think-aloud group were instructed to "talk out loud while they solved the problems, describing what they noticed and what hypotheses they were entertaining" (P. A. Carpenter et al., 1990, p. 410). While the results of statistical tests were not reported, the error rate of participants in the experimental (metacognitive think-aloud group) was said to be slightly higher than the control group. Furthermore, solution times were typically longer as error rates increased, so on average the metacognitive think-aloud group spent more time solving the problems than the control.

Reactivity for Accuracy but not for Latency

About 40 per cent of the studies reviewed (11 of the 30) found reactivity for accuracy but either did not report solution time or found verbalization not to affect solution time. Such lack of reporting is unfortunate, as it limits the conclusions that can be drawn from the research. Again, in some cases verbalization improved performance, whereas in others, it hindered task performance.

IMPROVED TASK PERFORMANCE

Bower and King (1967) investigated the effects of verbalization, sex, and number of irrelevant stimulus dimensions on a rule learning

Table 2.5 Studies Comparing Metacognitive Protocols and Silent Controls: Reactivity for Accuracy but not Latency

Study	Participants	Task(s)	Groups	Design	Reactivity	Non-Reactivity
Berry (1983)[a]	60 undergraduates at Hatfield Polytechnic	Wason's selection task	1. no verbalization (NV) 2. conc. TA + meta (CV) 3. retro TA + meta (PV) 4. two unrelated conditions	Between-subjects	Accuracy (for both + meta groups but effect stronger for concurrent group)	
Bower and King (1967)[a]	18 men attending Dalhousie University and 18 nursing students	Rule learning task	1. TA + meta 2. control (no verbalization)	Between-subjects	Accuracy (on first problem only)	
Davis, Carey, Foxman, & Tarr. (1968)[a]	48 college students in an introductory psychology course	Tower of Hanoi	1. solution set (rule search) 2. TA + meta	Between-subjects	Accuracy on transfer task	
Hagafors & Brehmer (1983)[a]	64 high school students	CPL task	1. feedback /justification 2. feedback /no justification 3. no feedback/ justification 4. no feedback/ no justification	Between-subjects	Accuracy in the no feedback condition	Accuracy in the feedback condition
McGeorge & Burton (1989, Exp. 1)[a]	35 undergraduates	Same tasks as Berry & Broadbent (1984)	1. silent control 2. TA + meta	Between-subjects	Accuracy (even without explanation of system)	
Short, Schatschneider, Cuddy, Evans,	94 bright, average, learning disabled, and	Spatial and verbal analogies	T1 = silent T2 = TA + meta	Within-subjects	Accuracy for all students on all analogies (most	

Study	Participants	Task	Conditions	Design	Measure	Measure
Dellick, & Basili (1991)[a]	developmentally handicapped fifth-graders				profound effects for bright and average students)	Latency
Schooler, Ohlsson, & Brooks (1993, Exp. 1)	86 college students	Insight problems	1. retrospective TA + meta 2. silent control	Between-subjects	Accuracy	
Stanley, Mathews, Buss, & Kotler-Cope (1989, Exp 1)[a]	77 undergraduates	Same tasks as Berry & Broadbent (1984)	1. TA + meta (sugar) 2. TA + meta (person) 3. silent control (sugar) 4. silent control (person)	Between-subjects	Accuracy on both tasks	
Stinessen (1985)[a]	40 undergraduate students	Tower of Hanoi	1. silent control 2. conc. TA + meta	Between-subjects	Accuracy	
Wilder & Harvey (1971)	30 17- and 18-year-old students	Tower of Hanoi	1. control (no verbalization) 2. overt + meta verbalization 3. covert + meta verbalization	Between-subjects	Accuracy (for both + meta groups)	Latency
Wilson & Schooler (1991)[a]	243 introductory psychology students	Ranking course preferences	1. silent control 2. rate all 3. TA + meta	Between-subjects	Accuracy	

Notes
T1 = time one; T2 = time two.
+ meta = metacognitive.
a Indicates that time was not reported.

task. Participants were 18 male university students and 18 female nursing school students. They were all presented with three successive problems (composed of 16 stimuli) possessing different relevant attributes based on the same underlying abstract classification rule. Participants were instructed to classify each stimulus into one of two binary categories. Half of the participants were instructed to verbalize hypotheses before making classifications while the other half were not asked to verbalize at all. Results indicated that the requirement to verbalize hypotheses improved performance significantly (reducing the mean number of errors), but only on the first problem. The effects may have been limited to the first problem because the act of verbalizing may have helped the participants ignore irrelevant features initially (Ericsson & Simon, 1993, p. 102).

J.H. Davis et al. (1968), building on the work of Gagné and Smith (1962), examined the effect of experimenter's presence on participants' performance on a Tower of Hanoi problem. Participants were 48 college students in an introductory psychology course. Like Gagné and Smith (1962), there were solution set groups (in which participants were instructed to formulate a rule after completing the problem) and verbalization groups (in which participants stated justifications for each move they made during the task). In addition, the variable of experimenter presence was added, to determine whether the act of verbalizing itself accounted for the positive effects on performance found in the earlier study, or whether the act of communicating and interacting with the experimenter played a role as well. Again, as in Gagné and Smith (1962), participants first completed a training task (a five-disk problem) and then a more complicated (six-disk) transfer task. Following the earlier study, verbalization was not required on the transfer task, but just on the training task. Results indicated that, unlike in Gagné and Smith (1962), verbalization did not have a significant effect on performance on the training task, although it did significantly reduce the number of moves needed to solve the transfer task. Conversely, experimenter's presence improved performance on the training task but not on the transfer task. No information about solution times was reported.

Wilder and Harvey (1971), again using Gagné and Smith's (1962) study as a point of departure, investigated the effects of covert verbalization on task performance with a Tower of Hanoi problem. Participants were 30 seventeen- and eighteen-year-old students attending a summer course in speech and journalism. None had previous experience with the Tower of Hanoi. The design followed that of Gagné and Smith (1962), with the participants first being introduced to the problem and its rules and then being assigned to one of three groups – (1) control (no verbalization), (2) overt verbalization, or (3) covert verbalization. Participants in the overt verbalization group were instructed:

> State out loud a full reason for each move as completely as you can . . . If you choose to back up at any point be sure to verbalize a reason for each move as you retrace your steps.
>
> (Wilder & Harvey, 1971, p. 173)

The covert verbalization group received the following instructions:

> Carefully consider each individual move. Think of a full reason for each move as if you were being asked to report your reasons out loud. Do not move until you feel confident there is a good reason for the move you are about to make. Remember to approach each move as if you were being required to state your reason out loud.
>
> (Wilder & Harvey, 1971, p. 173)

The control group averaged 27.32 excess moves on the six different problems, as compared to 12.88 excess moves for the overt verbalization group and 12.30 for the covert verbalization group. An ANOVA indicated that there was a significant main effect for condition, and Scheffé post-hoc comparisons revealed significant differences between the control group and both verbalization groups. No significant difference was found between the two verbalization groups, indicating that covert verbalization was as effective in improving task performance as overt verbalization. There was no significant difference between the verbalization and control group in terms of solution time. This finding is crucial, as it suggests that the positive effects of verbalization are not, at least in this case, due to extra time.

Stinessen (1985), again using the Tower of Hanoi task, investigated the effects of metacognitive verbalization on problem-solving performance. The 40 undergraduate student participants were all introduced to the task and shown how the three-disk problem could be solved. They were then randomly assigned to either the control (silent) condition or the concurrent metacognitive think-aloud condition, in which they were required to give reasons for every move they made. Results of an ANOVA showed a significant main effect for treatment, and the mean number of errors for participants in the verbalizing group was significantly lower than for the control group (6.0 as compared to 11.25). Therefore, results showed that stating reasons facilitated performance and reduced the occurrence of errors. Furthermore, post-hoc *t* tests indicated that this difference in performance was due to "a significant decrease in errors for moves close to important subgoals" that were crucial for successful task completion (Stinessen, 1985, p. 342). Time was not reported for either group in this study.

Berry and Broadbent (1984) investigated the relationship between verbalization and explanation of a system on participants' performance on two computerized tasks. In one task (sugar production), participants took on the role of manager of a sugar plant and had to maintain a certain level of sugar production by varying the number of employees. In a second task (personal interaction), participants interacted with a computerized "person" and had to maintain a certain level of intimacy. Twenty-four university students were assigned to either a control (silent) group or to a concurrent (metacognitive) think-aloud group. Results on both tasks indicated that the requirement to verbalize hypotheses and justifications alone did not improve performance but that performance did improve when participants were provided with a meaningful explanation of the system and specific variables that they could use to guide their thinking. Again, no report of time was provided.

McGeorge and Burton (1989) used the same tasks as in Berry and Broadbent (1984), but investigated the effect of concurrent (metacognitive) verbalization when there was no provision of organizing/explanatory information on task performance. In Experiment 1, 35 undergraduates were randomly assigned to either a control (no verbalization) or to a metacognitive verbalization group, in which students were asked to "verbalize and describe any heuristics they were following and the reasoning behind" each choice (McGeorge & Burton, 1989, p. 459). Results indicated that participants in the verbalization group performed significantly better on the task than the control group, even in the absence of a graphic representation of the system, as was provided in Berry and Broadbent (1984).

Stanley et al. (1989) again used the same tasks as Berry and Broadbent (1984), but this time they investigated the effects of a slightly different type of metacognitive verbalization (referred to as "teach-aloud") on task performance. In Experiment 1, 77 undergraduates were randomly assigned to one of four groups – (1) verbalization (sugar task), (2) verbalization (person task), (3) control (sugar task), or (4) control (person task). Participants in the control groups did not verbalize, whereas those in the verbalization groups were instructed to instruct an invisible partner how to complete the task as s/he completed each step. After the participants completed each step, they were prompted: "Please give your instructions for your partner. Try to be as complete and specific as possible in telling him or her how you are making your choices" (Stanley et al., 1989, p. 559). Results indicated that scores on both tasks were significantly higher for subjects in the verbalization condition than for those in the control condition. Therefore, the concurrent verbalization procedure was found to have significantly improved performance.

Short et al. (1991) examined the effect of concurrent metacognitive verbalization on solving a test of analogies in bright, average, learning disabled, and developmentally handicapped fifth-grade students. Ninety-four students randomly selected from three schools participated in the study. In the first session, all of the children took the Kaufman Assessment Battery for Children (a standardized test used to measure children's IQs). Then, in the second session, each child completed 11 spatial and 11 verbal analogies silently. Approximately three weeks later, in the final session, all of the children were instructed to complete the same analogies again, this time thinking aloud. In order to demonstrate how they wanted the children to think aloud, the researchers had each student practice thinking aloud about their favorite sport. Students were instructed: "Now pretend you had to tell a 6-year-old how to play the game. Tell me everything you think he or she would need to know in order to play the game" (Short et al., 1991, p. 143). Whenever the child's explanations were not explicit enough, the researcher prompted for more information with questions. After completing the practice trial, students were told:

> I want you to do the same thing again, only this time I want you to "think aloud" as you are solving these problems. Remember, tell me everything you are doing and thinking about as you are solving these problems.
>
> (Short et al., 1991, p. 143)

Furthermore, children were reminded at the outset of each problem to think aloud and were asked to explain why they chose each response as they chose it. Performance was analyzed using a repeated measures analysis of covariance (MANCOVA) with one between-subject factor (group), two within-subject factors (condition, silent vs. think-aloud) and problem type (spatial vs. verbal), and IQ as the covariate. A significant main effect was found for condition for all groups (bright, average, learning disabled, and developmentally handicapped). That is, all children performed significantly better on the analogies test in the think-aloud condition than in the silent condition. The most pronounced effects were found for the bright and average students, however. No mention of time was made, so it is not clear whether all groups spent an equal amount of time on the analogies.

HINDERED TASK PERFORMANCE

Berry (1983) investigated the effects of type of verbalization and feedback on performance in a Wason's selection task. Sixty undergraduates were randomly assigned to one of three verbalization groups – (1) no verbalization (NV), (2) concurrent (metacognitive) verbalization (CV), or (3) post retrospective (metacognitive) verbalization (PV), or to one of two unrelated conditions – (4) abstract minimal explanation (AME) or (5) abstract control (AC). Participants completed a series of practice trials and were then instructed on how they were to perform in the experimental trials. Those in the CV group were told:

> I am interested in the logical processes that you use to perform these tasks. On the next four trials I would like you to do your reasoning out loud. Please state your reasons for choosing or not choosing each of the jars/sleeves that you consider.
>
> (Berry, 1983, p. 43)

Participants in the PV group, in contrast, were not advised beforehand that they would be asked to provide justifications retrospectively. Results indicated that the CV and PV groups performed best, and the effect was most clearly seen on one set of trials, where the CV group achieved a score of 89.6 per cent correct, as compared to the PV group with 67.7 per cent correct and the NV and AC groups with dramatically lower scores of 27.1 per cent and 22.9 per cent, respectively. Time on task was not reported for any of the groups.

Wilson and Schooler (1991) investigated the effect of verbalizing justifications on course preferences among 243 introductory psychology students. All students received identical packets of information with details about course offerings for the following semester. Participants were then randomly assigned to one of three groups – (1) control, (2) rate all information, or (3) reasons condition. Participants in the control group ranked courses in order of preference without verbalizing and participants in the rate all group were instructed to evaluate the extent to which each detail affected their ranking. Participants in the reasons condition (concurrent metacognitive) were asked to "analyze why [they felt] the way they did about each course" and to write down their reasons for ranking a course a certain way (Wilson & Schooler, 1991, p. 187). All of the students' rankings were then compared to "expert" rankings. Results indicated that participants in both the rate all and reasons conditions ranked courses in a way that corresponded less with expert opinion, as compared to control participants. Wilson and Schooler hypothesize that the requirement to focus on justifications may cause participants to hone in on "non-optimal" criteria, thus causing the divergence from expert opinion.

Experiment 1 of Schooler et al. (1993) investigated the effects of metacognitive verbalization on the solution of insight problems by 86 undergraduates. Participants were randomly assigned to either a retrospective metacognitive verbalization group or to an "unrelated interruption" (control) group. All participants were given the same set of ten insight problems to solve, and after two minutes of working on the problems, all participants were interrupted and instructed to stop work. The period of interruption lasted one and a half minutes for both groups, but the instructions given to participants during that time differed for the two groups. Participants in the metacognitive verbalization group were instructed:

> Please stop working on the problem now and write down, in as much detail as possible, everything you can remember about how you have been trying to solve the problem. Give information about your approach, strategies, any solutions you tried, and so on.
>
> (Schooler et al., 1993, p. 170)

Participants in the control (unrelated interruption) condition, on the other hand, were instructed to work on a crossword puzzle during that time. *T* tests performed on the mean number of problems solved by participants in the two groups indicated that students in the verbalization condition correctly solved significantly fewer problems than those in the control group, suggesting that verbalization was reactive in this experiment, specifically hindering performance on this task. (Mean percentages correct were 35.6 per cent for the verbalization condition and 45.8 per cent for the unrelated interruption condition.) *T* tests performed on the mean amount of time taken to correctly solve the problems found no significant difference between the two groups, indicating that verbalization did not affect latency in this experiment.

Outliers

Two studies (U. Anderson & Wright, 1988; Hagafors & Brehmer, 1983) do not fit neatly into the patterns of results just discussed,

Table 2.6 Studies Comparing Metacognitive Protocols and Silent Controls: Outliers

Study	Participants	Task(s)	Groups	Design	Reactivity	Non-Reactivity
Anderson & Wright (1988)[a]	58 undergraduate accounting majors & 42 senior auditors	Risk assessment judgment	1) silent control 2) TA + meta	Between-subjects	Accuracy for novices	Accuracy for experts
Berry & Broadbent (1984)[a]	24 university students	Two computerized tasks: sugar production and personal interaction	1. silent control 2. conc. TA + meta	Between-subjects	Accuracy (only when subj. were provided with an explanation of the system)	

Note
+ meta = metacognitive.
a Indicates time was not reported.

since they found reactivity for accuracy for one group of participants but not for another, so these studies are discussed separately below.

Anderson and Wright (1988) examined the effects of verbalizing justifications on the perceived likelihood of an event. Two populations of participants – 58 undergraduate accounting majors and 42 senior auditors at a public accounting firm – took part in the study. All participants were told that they were to make a risk assessment judgment about a number of corporations, based on a series of facts they would receive. Participants were randomly assigned to either a control or to one of two treatment groups, and all received worksheets on which to record their judgments. The treatment group's worksheets differed from the control's, however, in that they prompted participants to provide concurrent metacognitive verbalizations. They were prompted: "Please write down in the space provided below any factors or reasons that would explain the occurrence of this event" and "List steps that could be taken to prevent the occurrence of this event" (U. Anderson & Wright, 1988, p. 261). Results of a MANCOVA indicated that metacognitive verbalization inflated the risk-oriented judgments only for the students (who represented novices in this experiment). Verbalization did not have any significant effect on the experienced auditors' judgments.

Hagafors and Brehmer (1983) investigated the effects of verbalized justification and feedback on performance on a cue-probability learning task. Sixty-four high school student participants were randomly assigned to (1) a feedback/justification group, (2) a feedback/no justification group, (3) a no feedback/justification group, or (4) a no feedback/no justification group. All participants completed a series of learning trials, followed by a similar experimental trial. Results indicated that verbal justification had a facilitative effect on task performance when no feedback was provided. When feedback was provided, no difference was found between justification and non-justification groups. In this case, then, reactivity was found for accuracy under one condition but not under another.

Reactivity for Latency but not for Accuracy

Three of the studies reviewed (Allwood, 1990; Fidler, 1983; K. M. Robinson, 2001) found reactivity for time (latency) but not for accuracy. That metacognitive protocols should show reactivity for time is not surprising, since it stands to reason that verbalizing justifications might require more time than (1) a verbalization not requiring such additional information or (2) no verbalization at all. However, as we have seen in the two previous sections, such reactivity for latency is

Table 2.7 Studies Comparing Metacognitive Protocols and Silent Controls: Reactivity for Latency but not Accuracy

Study	Participants	Task(s)	Groups	Design	Reactivity	Non-Reactivity
Allwood (1990, Exp 2)	40 students of first-year statistics	Two statistical problems	1. silent control 2. conc. TA + meta	Between-subjects	Time	Accuracy
Fidler (1983)	13 graduate business students	Single judgment task (predict future GPA)	1. silent control 2. conc. TA + meta 3. retro. TA + meta	Within-subjects	Time	Accuracy
K. M. Robinson (2001)	178 students in grades 1, 3, and 5	36 subtraction problems	1. silent control 2. retro. TA + meta 3. conc. TA + meta	Between-subjects	Time (slowest in all grades for conc. TA + meta)	Accuracy

Note
conc. TA + meta = concurrent metacognitive think-aloud.
retro. TA + meta = retrospective metacognitive think-aloud.

often accompanied by reactivity for accuracy (e.g. Ahlum-Heath & di Vesta, 1986; Berardi-Coletta et al., 1995; Brunk et al., 1958; P. A. Carpenter et al., 1990; Hafner, 1957).

Fidler (1983) examined the validity of verbal reports obtained in a single judgment task. In the study, 13 graduate business students were asked to predict future GPAs in business school for a certain group of undergraduates on the basis of a number of pieces of quantitative information, including the students' graduate management admission test (GMAT) scores and college GPAs. In a within-subjects design, participants made judgments in one of three conditions – (1) a silent condition, (2) concurrent think-aloud (metacognitive) condition, or (3) retrospective (metacognitive) think-aloud condition. The experiment was conducted in two sessions, one week apart. In each session half the decisions were made while thinking aloud and the other half were made silently. Additionally, the decisions that were verbalized in session 1 were made silently in session 2, and vice versa. In the concurrent condition, participants were told to

> verbalize every thought and every detail of their thinking process, including what information they were looking at, what thoughts they were having about any piece of information, how they were evaluating the different pieces of information, and the reasons which led to their decisions.
>
> (Fidler, 1983, p. 434)

In the retrospective condition, participants were first asked: "You just responded that alternative 1 [or] 2 would do better in graduate school. How did you reach this decision?" (Fidler, 1983, p. 434). Then, probing for more specific justifications, they were asked: "Which decision attributes were most important for this last decision?" (Fidler, 1983, p. 434). Results found no reliable differences in decision outcome between the groups. However, reactivity was found for latency, given that the average decision time of verbalized decisions (58.7 seconds) was more than double that of decisions made silently (24.7 seconds).

Allwood (1990, Study 2) examined the effects of providing verbal justifications for each step on a series of statistics problems. In the study, 40 students enrolled in a first-year statistics class were asked to solve two statistics problems. Students were randomly assigned either to a control (no verbalization) or to an experimental (metacognitive concurrent think-aloud) group. Participants in the experimental group received the following instructions regarding verbalization:

Please tell me which formula or formulae you consider using to solve [each] part of the problem. Before you decide finally which formula to use please give me a careful justification showing that the formula or the way you intend to use it is the correct one. The justification for your choice of formula should not be of the type "this formula is the best" or "this formula seems to be correct," but the justification should proceed from the meaning of the components of the formula and what you want to achieve. Accordingly, the justification should, based on the meaning of the components of the formula, make clear why you think the formula is the correct one to use.

(Allwood, 1990, p. 185)

The control group was given no instructions to verbalize. Results revealed that students' performance on the two problems was not affected by thinking aloud, since the verbalization group and control group's performance were statistically similar. Thus reactivity for accuracy was not found. However, reactivity for latency (solution time) was found: the average time to complete the first problem for the control group was 32 minutes, as compared to an average of 42 minutes for the experimental group. Similarly, the average time to complete the second problem for the control group was 23 minutes, as compared to 33 minutes for the experimental group.

Robinson (2001) investigated the effects of type of verbal report on children's accuracy in solving subtraction problems. One hundred and seventy-eight students in grades 1, 3, and 5 were asked to solve the same 36 subtraction problems without receiving any feedback. Students were randomly assigned to one of three conditions – (1) the no report (NR) condition, (2) retrospective (metacognitive) report (RR) condition, or (3) concurrent (metacognitive) report (CR) condition. Students in the NR condition were told: "We are going to do some subtraction problems today. I'll show a problem to you, and when you have an answer, tell me what it is. You can do anything you want to get the right answer" (K. M. Robinson, 2001, p. 213). Those in the RR condition received the above instructions and then after solving the first problem were asked: "I'm really interested in how kids your age figure out the answers to these problems. How did you figure out the answer to that problem?" (K. M. Robinson, 2001, p. 213). Students in the CR condition received the same instructions as the NR condition but before solving the first problem were told:

I'm really interested in how kids your age figure out the answers to these problems. I'll show a problem to you, and I want you to tell me how you are trying to figure out the answer while you are working on the problem.

(K. M. Robinson, 2001, p. 213)

Both accuracy and latency were examined. Mean accuracy scores were compared as a function of grade (1, 3, or 5) and report condition (NR, RR, or CR), and no significant differences were found between report conditions for any grade, thus indicating that verbalization did not affect performance in this study. Mean latencies were also compared across grades and report conditions, and latencies were slowest for the CR condition in all grades.

Reactivity for Neither Latency nor Accuracy

Four of the studies reviewed (Biehal & Chakravarti, 1989; Brehmer et al., 1974; Evans et al., 1983; Mathews et al., 1989) found reactivity for neither time nor accuracy; that is, their results showed that thinking aloud had no effect on solution time or task performance. The fact that metacognitive reports did not increase solution latency in these studies is surprising, although as we will see, this could be due to the type of task. In accordance with the predictions of Ericsson and Simon's (1993) model, if the task itself leads participants to think through justifications, then the mere act of verbalizing those justifications should cause minimal interference and/or increased latency.

Brehmer et al. (1974) used a probabilistic inference task to study the effects of verbalizing justifications on performance. One hundred twenty-eight students were assigned to either a control (no verbalization) or experimental (concurrent metacognitive verbalization) group. Students in the experimental group were asked to verbalize their hypotheses as they worked through the task while the control group did not verbalize at all. Results indicated that the requirement to verbalize hypotheses did not affect the learning of the task.

Experiment 2 of Evans et al. (1983) investigated the effect of verbalization on performance on syllogistic reasoning problems. In the study 64 undergraduates were randomly assigned to either a silent (control) group, retrospective (metacognitive) think-aloud condition or a concurrent (metacognitive) think-aloud condition. In both think-aloud conditions, participants were instructed to answer each of the four problems and "explain why [they] believe the conclusion to be valid or invalid as the case may be" (Evans et al., 1983, p. 298). Evans et al. (1983) then performed a series of 2 × 4 Chi-square tests to compare response frequencies across the groups for

Table 2.8 Studies Comparing Metacognitive Protocols and Silent Controls: Reactivity for Neither Latency nor Accuracy

Study	Participants	Task(s)	Groups	Design	Reactivity	Non-Reactivity
Biehal & Chakravarti (1989)[a]	62 college students (82% undergrads, 18% graduates and secretaries)	Brand decision task	*1st decision task* 1. concurrent TA + meta 2. silent *2nd decision task* All concurrent TA + meta	Between-subjects		Choice outcomes (brand decision)
Brehmer (1974)[a]	64 undergraduate students of psychology	CPL task	1. TA − meta 2. TA + meta	Between-subjects		Accuracy
Evans, Barston, & Pollard (1983, Exp 2)[a]	64 undergraduates	Syllogistic reasoning problems	1. control (silent) 2. retro TA + meta 3. conc TA + meta	Between-subjects		Accuracy
Mathews, Buss, Stanley, Blanchard-Fields, Cho, & Druhan (1989, Exp 2)[a]	168 undergraduates	Artificial grammar activities	1. T1 & T2 silent 2. T1 & T2 (TA + meta) All verbalized at T3	Between-subjects		Accuracy

Note
a Indicates that time was not reported.

the four problems. No significant differences were found among the groups and time was not reported.

Experiment 2 of Mathews et al. (1989) investigated the reactive effects of the verbalization procedure used in Stanley et al.(1989), which was deemed "teach-aloud." In the study, 168 undergraduate students completed two sessions of activities in which they learned an artificial grammar, and in a third session they verbalized their knowledge to a partner. These verbalizations were compared to verbalizations by students who had verbalized using the teach-aloud procedure during the first two sessions as well. Results indicated that "Week 3 verbalizations show[ed] levels of accessibility to implicit knowledge of grammar similar to that found in Experiment 1," thus indicating that the accessible knowledge is not an artifact of verbalization during Weeks 1 and 2 (Mathews et al., 1989, p. 1092).

Framed in a different context, Biehal and Chakravarti (1989) investigated the reactivity of concurrent metacognitive protocols in consumer information processing. In their study, 62 participants, mostly college students, completed two brand decision tasks. Participants were randomly assigned to either the metacognitive concurrent verbalization group or to a silent control group. Both groups completed a warm-up task in which they were asked:

> Cast your mind back to the last time you made an apartment or housing choice. Please take about 5 minutes to describe out loud what you can remember about the decision process you followed at that time. For instance talk about the apartments or houses you looked at, factors important to you, why you rejected the ones you did, people who influenced your final choice, etc.
> (Biehal & Chakravarti, 1989, p. 95)

Then participants completed the first decision task, in which they were asked to choose one of eight pocket calculators to buy for a friend based on a matrix of attributes. Participants in the verbalization group were instructed to "describe out loud [their] thoughts, as much as [they] did before with the apartments" (Biehal & Chakravarti, 1989, p. 95). Participants in the control group were not instructed to verbalize at all. All participants then completed a second decision task, in which they were provided with additional information about the brands of calculators. In this trial, participants in both groups performed concurrent metacognitive verbalization while making their decision. Chi-square tests indicated that there was no significant difference between percentages of participants in each group who chose each brand of calculator. The authors therefore conclude that neither the first nor the second decision out-comes were affected by verbalization, indicating that verbalization was not reactive in this situation. Time was not reported for either group.

Studies Comparing Metacognitive and Non-Metacognitive Protocols

Ericsson and Simon (1993), in their review of studies involving metacognitive verbalization, find mixed results with regard to reactivity. The majority of the studies surveyed examine the effects of metacognitive think-alouds versus a silent control group, finding metacognitive think-alouds to be reactive for accuracy in most cases (e.g. Berry, 1983; Berry & Broadbent, 1984; Bower & King, 1967; J. H. Davis et al., 1968; McGeorge & Burton, 1989; Short et al., 1991; Stanley et al., 1989; Wilder & Harvey, 1971; Wilson & Schooler, 1991). For many of the studies, time (latency) is not reported, but Ericsson and Simon's (1993) prediction that metacognitive verbalization requires extra processing time as compared to other types of verbalizations or to a control, is borne out in almost all of the studies that do report latency (e.g. Ahlum-Heath & di Vesta, 1986; Allwood, 1990; P. A. Carpenter et al., 1990; Fidler, 1983; Gagné & Smith, 1962; K. M. Robinson, 2001). Ericsson and Simon (1993) review only a handful of empirical studies that directly compare metacognitive and non-metacognitive think-alouds in terms of reactivity, however. A thorough search in the literature revealed several more relevant studies, many of which were published after Ericsson and Simon's (1993) book. The results of all of these studies (see Tables 2.9 through 2.11) are briefly summarized below.

Reactivity for Accuracy

IMPROVED TASK PERFORMANCE

In a series of four experiments, Berardi-Coletta et al.(1995) investigated the effects of verbalization on solution transfer in two problem-solving tasks, the Tower of Hanoi and the Katona card problem. In Experiment 1, 109 undergraduates were randomly assigned to solve the Tower of Hanoi in one of five groups – (1) metacognitive, (2) if-then, (3) problem-focused, (4) think-aloud, or (5) silent (control). Each participant, regardless of condition, was first trained on the two, three, four, and five-disk versions of the Tower of Hanoi task and then presented with the six-disk version to solve as a

Table 2.9 Studies Comparing Non-Metacognitive and Metacognitive Protocols: Reactivity for Accuracy

Study	Participants	Task(s)	Groups	Design	Reactivity	Non-Reactivity
Berardi-Coletta, Buyer, Dominowski, & Rellinger (1995)	Exp 1: 109 undergraduates Exp 2: 64 undergraduates Exp 3: 40 undergraduates. Exp 4: 15 undergraduates	Exp 1: Tower of Hanoi Exp 2: Katona card problem Exp 3: Tower of Hanoi Exp 4: Katona card problem	Exp 1: 2 TA + meta groups, 2 TA – meta groups, 1 control (silent) Exp 2: 1 TA + meta group, 1 TA – meta group, 1 control (silent) Exp 3: TA + meta or control (silent) Exp 4: TA + meta or TA – meta	Between-subjects	Accuracy and time	
Brunk, Collister, Swift, & Stayton (1958)	147 undergraduate students	Two Vygotsky tests (Ladd test and PAMS test)	1. concurrent non-metacognitive verbalization 2. concurrent metacognitive verbalization	Between-subjects	Accuracy[b] (% of forest saved)[b]	
Dickson, McLennan, & Omodei (2000)[a]	60 undergraduates	Computerized forest-fire fighting simulator	1. control (silent) 2. TA – meta 3. TA + meta	Between-subjects	Accuracy and time	No. of decision actions taken

Notes
+ meta = metacognitive.
– meta = non-metacognitive.
a Indicates that time was not reported.
b The metacognitive verbalization group performed significantly worse than the control group; the non-metacognitive verbalization group performed between the two extremes, only slightly worse in terms of accuracy than the control.

transfer task. Participants were instructed to verbalize during the training tasks but not during the six-disk transfer task. Verbalization instructions varied according to condition. The metacognitive group was asked one of the following questions before each move:

1. How are you deciding which disk to move next?
2. How are you deciding where to move the next disk?
3. How do you know that this is a good move?

The if-then group received the following instructions:

> Before each move, I want you to tell me where you are going to move each disk, and why. Specifically, I want you to state this in an "if-then" statement, for example, "if I move this disk to this peg, then this will happen."
>
> (Berardi-Coletta et al., 1995, p. 207).

The problem-focused group was asked one of the following questions before each move:

1. What is the goal of the problem?
2. What are the rules of the problem?
3. What is the current state of the problem (where are the disks right now)?

The think-aloud group was instructed to simply "think out loud while you are solving this problem. Try to keep talking as much as you can so that I can hear what you are thinking about as you solve the problem" (Berardi-Coletta et al., 1995, p. 207). In summary, there were two metacognitive groups (the metacognitive and if-then groups) and two non-metacognitive groups (problem-focused and think-aloud groups). Results of a repeated measures ANOVA indicated that the metacognitive (metacognitive and if-then) groups had superior performance compared to the other groups. Therefore, the positive effects of verbalization on solution transfer were attributed to the requirement "to produce verbalizations that forced [participants] to shift their focus to the processing level" (Berardi-Coletta et al., 1995, p. 210). The metacognitive and if-then groups also spent more time on average per move (6.2 and 7.8 seconds, respectively) than the other groups (approximately 5 seconds).

Experiment 2 was designed to test whether the results of the first experiment could be generalized to a problem-solving task of a different type (a structure-inducing task), the Katona card problem. At the beginning of the task, the researcher deals eight playing cards (Ace, 2, 3, 4, 5, 6, 7, and 8). The first is dealt face-up on the table and the second face-down, placed at the bottom of the deck. The third card is dealt face-up on the table, and the fourth face-down, again placed on the bottom of the deck. The pattern repeats until all the cards have been dealt face-up on the table. The problem-solver's task is to figure out the order in which the cards have to be arranged at the outset so that as the cards are dealt, they will appear in numerical order, beginning with the Ace.

In the study, 64 undergraduates were randomly assigned to one of three groups – (1) metacognitive, (2) problem-focused, or (3) silent (control). As in the first experiment, participants were asked to verbalize during a series of simpler training tasks but not during the transfer task itself. Participants in the metacognitive group were asked one of the following questions, according to their progress on the task:

1. What are you thinking about in terms of starting to solve this problem? (asked at the beginning of a trial)
2. How are you deciding on a way to work out the order for the cards? Or, how are you working out the order for the cards? (asked when participants pause in writing down their solution)
3. How did you decide that this needed to be changed? (asked when participants changed their solution)
4. How are you deciding what went wrong? (asked following an unsuccessful trial)

Participants in the problem-focused group were asked one of the following questions:

1. What is the goal of the problem?
2. What is the dealing rule of the problem?
3. What cards do you have in order thus far?

Participants in the silent (control) group were not instructed to verbalize at all. Thus, there was one metacognitive group (the metacognitive group), one non-metacognitive group (the problem-focused group), and one silent group. Results for accuracy were consistent with those of Experiment 1, indicating that the metacognitive (metacognitive) group performed significantly better than the other groups on the transfer task. Again, as in Experiment 1, reactivity for time was found, but this time the metacognitive group solved the problems in less time than the other groups, potentially because the metacognitive group required fewer trials on average to solve the problem.

Experiment 3 was also conducted to build on Experiment 1, testing the hypothesis of independence of verbalization and metacognitive processing. The Tower of Hanoi task was used, and 40 undergraduates were assigned to either a metacognitive (metacognitive think aloud) or silent (control) group. The participants in the metacognitive group were instructed to verbalize in the same way as in Experiment 1, during a series of practice tasks. No verbalization was required during the transfer task. Reactivity was again found for accuracy on the transfer task, as the experimental group made slightly more than one error move for every correct move, as compared to 2.5 error moves for every correct move for the control group. In terms of time, the experimental group consistently spent more time on each move in the practice tasks than the control, but then on the transfer task the trend shifted sharply with the control group taking about 35 per cent more time than the experimental group to solve the problem.

In Experiment 4, the Katona card problem was used and 15 undergraduates were randomly assigned to either the metacognitive (metacognitive) or think-aloud (non-metacognitive) group. As in the earlier experiments, participants verbalized during practice tasks but not during the transfer task. Instructions given to the metacognitive group were identical to those in Experiment 2, and participants in the think-aloud group were simply instructed to think out loud and talk as much as they could while completing the task. Results again indicated reactivity for accuracy, as significantly more participants in the metacognitive (metacognitive) group solved the transfer task correctly than the think-aloud (non-metacognitive) group. Again, reactivity for time was found. The think-aloud group took approximately twice as long as the metacognitive group to solve the three most difficult problems on the transfer task, and the metacognitive group required more time than the think-aloud group to solve the two easier problems. This is not unexpected, since the justification for the simpler problems could have slowed down the metacognitive group while simultaneously enhancing their performance on the more difficult problems.

HINDERED TASK PERFORMANCE

In Brunk et al. (1958), the earliest study found investigating the reactive effects of metacognitive versus non-metacognitive protocols, 147 undergraduate students were given an initial Vygotsky-type test (the Ladd test) and then a second, similar test (the PAMS test). All students completed the first test under normal administration (silent) conditions, but for the second test students were randomly assigned to either a control (non-metacognitive verbalization) or a concurrent metacognitive condition. In the metacognitive condition, during each task participants were "requested to tell why [they] placed each block where [they] did and were encouraged to verbalize freely" (Brunk et al., 1958, p. 238). The correlation between scores on the first and second tests was significantly lower under the concurrent metacognitive think-aloud condition than under the non-metacognitive condition. Therefore, the results suggest that requiring the participants to verbalize justifications as they completed the second test hindered their performance. Also, participants in the justification condition took longer to solve the PAMS test than did participants not required to provide such reasoning.

Dickson et al. (2000) investigated the effects of metacognitive and non-metacognitive concurrent verbalization on performance using a time-critical, dynamic decision-making task. Sixty undergraduate students were trained on how to use Fire Chief, a computerized forest fire-fighting simulator. Participants played the role of a fire chief and attempted to control a forest fire by deploying various types of fire-fighting equipment. After receiving training on how to use the software, participants were randomly assigned to one of three conditions – (1) control (silent), (2) associative verbalization (non-metacognitive think-aloud), or (3) procedural verbalization (metacognitive think-aloud). Participants in the control condition completed the simulation silently, as they had during training sessions. Participants in the associative verbalization condition were instructed "to think aloud during each trial, putting into words whatever was in their mind as they took each decision action" but were expressly told not to explain the reasons for their actions (Dickson et al., 2000, p. 222). Conversely, participants in the procedural verbalization condition were instructed to "put into words the basis of each decision action" (Dickson et al., 2000, p. 222). All participants completed two experimental trials, one immediately after the other. A MANCOVA was used to analyze the effects of verbalization on performance. The independent variable was verbalization condition and the dependent variables were (1) mean percentage of the forest saved and (2) mean number of decision actions across the two trials. Results indicated a significant main effect for verbalization condition on the first dependent variable, percentage of forest saved. Univariate F tests further indicated the source of the main effect (mean percentage of forest saved was 57.7 per cent in the control group, as compared to 52.6 per cent and 46.5 per cent in the associative and procedural verbalization groups, respectively). However, verbalization did not have a significant effect on mean number of decision actions taken. That is, the requirement to verbalize negatively affected performance but did not alter the number of decisions that participants were able to make in the time period set for the simulation (which was constant for all groups). Specifically, participants in the procedural verbalization (metacognitive) condition performed significantly worse than participants in the control (silent) condition, whereas participants in the associative verbalization condition (non-metacognitive) performed only slightly worse than the control group in terms of the amount of forest land they were able to save from fire in the simulation. In this case, both non-metacognitive and metacognitive verbalization were found to be reactive for accuracy, although metacognitive verbalization was found to be reactive to a greater degree. Since this result is not duplicated by other studies, it stands to reason that task type could be an important variable to consider.

Non-Reactivity for Accuracy

In Brehmer (1974), 64 undergraduate students of psychology were asked to complete a cue-probability learning (CPL) task, making predictions along the way to assist them in inferring the value of a criterion variable from that of a cue variable. The control group verbalized only their predictions, whereas the experimental group was asked to describe the rule they used to arrive at each prediction. The description was to be explicit enough that another participant could understand and use the rule themselves; if the description was not clear enough, the experimenter prompted for more information. An ANOVA showed no significant effect or interactions associated with type of verbalization and time was not reported. Brehmer therefore concluded that participants were able to report their hypotheses in this type of task without interfering with performance. Ericsson and Simon (1993) further temper these results, however, suggesting that the CPL task in this study involved such simple stimuli that it might not have been a valid test for reactivity (Brehmer, 1974, p. 102).

S. P. Norris (1990) examined five groups of students taking a test of critical thinking (Part A of the test for appraising observations). Participants were 343 high school students randomly assigned to either (1) a silent (control) group, (2) a concurrent (non-metacognitive) think-aloud group, (3) an immediate recall (metacognitive) group, or (4) a criteria or principle probe elicitation group (in which participants, after choosing an answer to each problem, were asked specific questions probing them for metacognitive information). An ANOVA revealed that there were no statistically significant

Table 2.10 Studies Comparing Non-Metacognitive and Metacognitive Protocols: Non-Reactivity for Accuracy

Study	Participants	Task(s)	Groups	Design	Reactivity	Non-Reactivity
Brehmer et al. (1974)[a]	128 undergraduates	Probabilistic inference task	1. control (silent) 2. conc. TA + meta	Between-subjects		Accuracy
S. P. Norris (1990)[a]	343 high school students	Multiple-choice test of critical thinking (Part A of the test for appraising observations)	1. control (silent) 2. conc. TA – meta 3. imm. recall TA + meta 4. criteria or probe TA + meta	Between-subjects		Accuracy

Note
conc. TA = concurrent think-aloud
imm. recall = immediate recall
+ meta = metacognitive
– meta = non-metacognitive.
a Indicates that time was not reported.

differences in performance (test scores) between any of the groups. Subsequent qualitative and quantitative analysis of the protocols from the different groups further revealed "little systematic difference between the elicitation groups" (S. P. Norris, 1990, p. 51). Norris took these findings to mean that "the elicitation of verbal reports of thinking did not alter subjects' performance and, by inference, did not alter their thinking; and the different procedures for eliciting verbal reports yielded essentially the same information of the quality of subjects' thinking" (S. P. Norris, 1990, p. 47). Again, however, time on task was not reported.

Mixed Results for Reactivity

Russo et al. (1989) set out to investigate the reactivity and veridicality of various types of verbal reports. Three report conditions were examined – (1) a silent control condition, (2) a concurrent condition, and (3) a retrospective condition. Participants' eye movements were also tracked and recorded during the experiment. Participants in the concurrent condition were instructed simply to "think aloud while solving the problem[s]," a seemingly non-metacognitive instruction (Russo et al., 1989, p. 761). In the retrospective condition, a metacognitive protocol was elicited, as participants were asked to "explain why [they] looked where [they] looked and what [they] were thinking when [they] looked there" (Russo et al., 1989, p. 761). In a repeated-measures design, 24 participants were asked to solve four different types of problem-solving tasks – a mathematical task (mental addition), a verbal task (anagrams), a numerical task (gambles), and a pictorial task (Raven's Progressive Matrices), each in a different condition. All participants received training on the protocol methods before completing the experimental tasks. Results differed for the four tasks, indicating that concurrent (non-metacognitive) verbalization significantly improved accuracy on the gambles and significantly decreased accuracy on addition. There were no reliable differences found between the concurrent and control groups on either the anagrams or the Raven's matrices. Reactivity for latency was found for the concurrent group, as response times were increased by 22–44 per cent over the control group, depending on the task. Similar analysis of the effects of retrospective protocols replicated the results of the concurrent group, further "suggesting that the causes of reactivity are not general but due jointly to the demands of the task and to verbalization" (Russo et al., 1989, p. 763).

This point made by Russo et al. (1989) is reiterated in Ericsson and Simon's (1993) book, which suggests that task requirements may

Table 2.11 Studies Comparing Non-Metacognitive and Metacognitive Protocols: Mixed Results for Reactivity

Study	Participants	Task(s)	Groups	Design	Reactivity	Non-Reactivity
Russo, Johnson, & Stephens (1989)	24 undergraduates	1. Mathematical task (mental addition) 2. Verbal task (anagrams) 3. Numerical task (gambles) 4. Pictorial task (Raven's matrices)	1. control (silent) 2. conc. TA – meta 3. retro. TA + meta	Between-subjects	Accuracy for both TA +/- meta on gambles and addition; Time for conc. group	Accuracy for both TA +/- meta on anagrams and Raven's matrices

Note
conc. TA = concurrent think-aloud
retro. TA = retrospective think-aloud
+ meta = metacognitive
– meta = non-metacognitive.

have a crucial impact on the reactivity (or lack thereof) of metacognitive verbalization: If justifications and explanations common to metacognitive verbalization are "generated as part of the normal process of solution," the mere act of verbalizing (metacognitive or not) should not have an effect on task performance (Ericsson & Simon, 1993, p. xxxiii). Given the variety of task types in the studies reviewed, it should not be surprising, then, that the findings are not unanimous regarding reactivity.

Conclusions

Based on the theoretical model proposed by Ericsson and Simon (1993) and the empirical evidence reported in this section, it is possible to draw some conclusions. Since the 1940s, verbal protocols have been used in fields such as cognitive psychology to probe cognitive processes. Theoretical models predict that verbalization of thoughts per se (what Ericsson and Simon refer to as Type 1 verbalizations, or non-metacognitive verbalizations) will be largely non-reactive; that is, they will reflect the nature of cognitive processes fairly accurately, while slowing processing slightly. Furthermore, models predict that verbalization of justifications (what Ericsson and Simon refer to as Type 2 and 3 verbalizations, or metacognitive verbalizations) may be more reactive. In many of the studies reported here, these predictions are supported, although some effects of task type have been shown (e.g. Deffner, 1989; Ericsson, 2002; Russo et al., 1989).

However, most of the studies reviewed employed non-verbal and/or problem-solving tasks, limiting their relevance to SLA. In fact, of all of the studies on reactivity found in the literature, only six used verbal tasks (Lass et al., 1991; Mathews et al., 1989; Rhenius & Deffner, 1990; Russo et al., 1989; Short et al., 1991; Stratman & Hamp-Lyons, 1994). For a brief overview of the methodologies of these studies, readers are referred back to Table 2.2. Of the six studies, only one (Short et al., 1991) found verbalization (in this case metacognitive) to be reactive for accuracy. However, these studies show great heterogeneity in terms of task type, with experimental tasks ranging from anagrams and verbal analogies to sentence assembly, text revision, and artificial grammar activities. Furthermore, they include participants from diverse pools, ranging from elementary school children to college-age students. As such, conclusive results cannot be taken from this small sample of studies with regard to reactivity of verbal reports on L1 verbal tasks, although the results in general support the finding of non-reactivity exhibited by non-verbal tasks, as shown in Table 2.12.

Table 2.12 Reactivity Studies from Cognitive Psychology Employing Verbal Tasks

Study	Participants	Task(s)	Groups	Design	Reactivity	Non-Reactivity
Lass, Klettke, Lüer, & Ruhlender (1991)	70 undergraduates	Anagrams	1. TA (− meta) 2. silent	Between-subjects	Latency	Accuracy
Mathews, Buss, Stanley, Blanchard-Fields, Cho, & Druhan (1989, Exp. 2)[a]	168 undergraduates	Artificial grammar activities	1. T1 & T2 silent 2. T1 & T2 (TA + meta) T3 – All verbalized	Between-subjects		Accuracy
Rhenius & Deffner (1990)	1. 24 students 2. 48 students 3. 21 students	1. sentence assembly 2. word puzzles and geometrical puzzles 3. Raven's matrices	1. TA (− meta) 2. silent	Between-subjects	Latency[b]	Accuracy
Russo, Johnson, & Stephens (1989)	24 undergraduates	1. Mental addition 2. Verbal task 3. Numerical task 4. Pictorial task	1) control (silent) 2) conc. TA − meta 3) retro. TA + meta	Between-subjects	Accuracy for both TA +/− meta on gambles and addition; Time for conc. group	Accuracy for both TA +/− meta on anagrams and Ravens matrices

Study	Participants	Task(s)	Groups	Design	Reactivity	Non-Reactivity
Short, Schatschneider, Cuddy, Evans, Dellick, & Basili (1991)*	94 bright, average., learning disabled, and developmentally handicapped fifth-graders	Spatial and verbal analogies	T1 – silent T2 – TA + meta	Within-subjects	Accuracy for all students on both types of analogies (most profound effects for bright and average students)	
Stratman and Hamp-Lyons (1994)	12 undergraduate and graduate students	Revision of text	1. TA – meta 2. silent	Within and between-subjects	No statistical analysis[b]	No statistical analysis

Notes

T1 = time one; T2 = time two; T3 = time three.

a Indicates that time was not reported.

b The metacognitive verbalization group performed significantly worse than the control group; the non-metacognitive verbalization group performed between the two extremes, only slightly worse in terms of accuracy than the control.

Synthesis: What Makes a Task Amenable to Thinking Aloud

As discussed in the previous section, it has been suggested "that the causes of reactivity are not general but due jointly to the demands of the task and to verbalization" (Russo et al., 1989, p. 763). This point is reiterated in Ericsson and Simon (1993), which suggests that task requirements may have a crucial impact on the reactivity (or lack thereof) of verbalization: If justifications and/or explanations common to verbalization are "generated as part of the normal process of solution," the mere act of verbalizing (metacognitive or not) should not have an effect on task performance (Ericsson & Simon, 1993, p. xxxiii). This is a good starting point to discuss what features make a task amenable to thinking aloud; however, it is certainly not the final word.

This literature review has primarily examined studies in the field of cognitive psychology, where much of the research to date on the validity of verbalization has occurred. Because most of the tasks are non-verbal in nature, the applicability of these studies' findings to SLA research is limited. Nevertheless, a number of generalizations can be taken from the body of research. Table 2.13 presents a list of all of the tasks used in the studies on reactivity examined in this chapter. Each task is listed as being either reactive or non-reactive, and the number in the column to the right of each task indicates the number of studies for which that finding of reactivity (or non-reactivity) was true. Although there is a diversity of tasks, 32 in all, a careful analysis reveals aspects of the tasks that make them more or less amenable to concurrent verbalization.

Looking at Table 2.13, it becomes apparent that there are two tasks that were used in multiple studies with the same pattern of findings regarding reactivity – (1) the Tower of Hanoi and (2) the sugar production and personal interaction simulators. Since both of these tasks were found to be reactive in all studies with all groups of participants, it stands to reason that the features of these tasks may make them unsuitable for verbalization. These tasks are examined in detail below.

Same Task, Same Results

The most obvious place to start is with the Tower of Hanoi problem, which was used in six of the studies reviewed. In all six cases, verbalization was reactive; that is, it affected performance on the problem. Invented by French mathematician Edouard Lucas in 1883, the Tower of Hanoi (see Figure 2.2) consists of a tower of eight disks,

Table 2.13 Tasks in Non-SLA Reactivity Studies

Non-reactive	N
Anagrams	2
Artificial grammar task	1
Brand decision	1
Critical thinking test	1
Cue-probability learning (CPL) task[a]	1
Investment analysis	1
Logic problems	1
Probabilistic inference task	1
Problem-solving in a faulty network	1
Raven's Matrices[b]	3
Sentence assembly	1
Simulated soccer games	1
Single judgment task (GPA prediction)	1
Statistical problems	1
Subtraction	1
Syllogistic reasoning task	1
Temperature regulation simulation	1
Word and geometrical puzzles	1

Reactive	
Addition	1
Cue-probability learning (CPL) task[a]	1
Forest fire-fighting	1
gambles	1
Insight problems	1
Katona card problem	1
Ranking course preferences	1
Raven's Matrices[b]	1
Rule learning task	1
Spatial/verbal analogies	1
Stencil test	1
Sugar production and personal interaction simulation	3
Tower of Hanoi	6
Valuation of equity firms	1
Vygotsky tests	1
Wason's selection task	1

Notes
a A CPL task was used in two studies, with verbalization being reactive in one and non-reactive in the other, so it is listed in both sections of the table.
b Raven's Matrices were used in four studies, with verbalization being reactive in one and non-reactive in the other three, so it is listed in both sections of the table.

initially stacked in increasing size on one of three pegs. The objective is to transfer the entire tower to one of the other pegs, moving only one disk at a time and never moving a larger disk onto a smaller one.

The solution to the problem is complex, as it involves both recursive functions and stacks and recurrence relations. It is a task that is frequently given to computer scientists and programmers, and solving it without the aid of a computer is quite daunting.

Three studies (Berry & Broadbent, 1984; McGeorge & Burton, 1989; Stanley et al., 1989) used the same set of tasks, developed by Berry and Broadbent (1984), which were two computer simulation tasks. In one task (sugar production) participants played the role of manager of a sugar plant and had to maintain a certain level of sugar production by varying the number of employees. In a second task (personal interaction) participants had to interact with a computerized "person" and maintain a certain level of intimacy. In all three studies, verbalization was found to be reactive. These tasks are reminiscent of the forest fire-fighting simulator used in Dickson et al. (2000) in the sense that they both require participants to make many decisions based on a multitude of factors.

Next, the table reveals that two tasks were used in multiple studies, with different patterns of results regarding reactivity. These are cue-probability learning (CPL) tasks, found to be non-reactive in one study and reactive in another, and Raven's Matrices, found to be non-reactive in three studies and reactive in one. A careful comparison of these studies can perhaps lead to an explanation of the differing findings and give some insight into the nature of reactivity with these tasks.

Same Task, Different Results

Notably, CPL tasks were used in two studies, with opposite findings regarding reactivity. In Hagafors and Brehmer (1983), participants were asked to complete a series of learning trials, followed by a similar experimental trial in which they had to infer the value of a criterion variable from that of a cue variable. They found verbalization to be reactive, whereas in Brehmer (1974) there was a finding of non-reactivity for a CPL task. A comparison of the two CPL tasks sheds some light on the differing findings. Brehmer himself suggests that the CPL task in the 1974 study involved such simple stimuli that it might not have been a valid test for reactivity (Brehmer, 1974, p. 102). In contrast, the CPL task used in Hagafors and Brehmer (1983) was much more complex, involving multiple cues and requiring more complex reasoning to arrive at a solution. Viewed from this perspective, the finding of non-reactivity for Brehmer (1974) is unsurprising, since it follows the established pattern that verbalization tends not to be reactive with simpler, less cognitively demanding tasks.

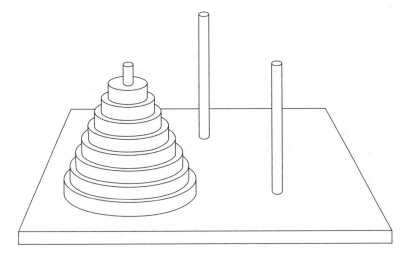

Figure 2.2 Tower of Hanoi

A task used in four of the studies reviewed (the Raven's Progressive Matrices Test) is worth mentioning, since non-reactivity was found in three of the studies and reactivity in the fourth. In this case, the same task was used with similar groups of participants in all cases, the only difference being that in the study that found reactivity (P. A. Carpenter et al., 1990) no statistical analyses were performed. In addition, the sample size in this study was small, consisting of just 12 participants, suggesting that even if the researcher had used inferential statistical tests, there might not have been enough statistical power to detect any significant differences between groups.

Similar Tasks, Different Results

Another interesting comparison can be made between two simple mathematical problem-solving tasks – subtraction in K. M. Robinson (2001), which was found to be non-reactive, and addition in Russo et al. (1989), which was found to be reactive. On the surface, this seems counterintuitive. How can two mathematical operations that are the converse of each other yield such different results with regard to reactivity? Looking at the studies more carefully, the difference in the two tasks becomes apparent. In the non-reactive case (K. M. Robinson's (2001) study), participants completed subtraction problems with the aid of paper and pencil while they verbally explained how they calculated their answers. In the reactive case (Russo et al., 1989), participants had to do addition problems "in their heads" (i.e. without writing anything down as they performed the calculations) and explain how they were arriving at their answers. Clearly, doing mathematical calculations mentally is more cognitively demanding than working the same problems with the aid of paper and pencil, writing as you calculate, in part perhaps because of constraints on working memory (Baddeley, 1986). So it seems that the less cognitively demanding task that placed fewer demands on working memory was less affected by verbalization.

Finally, an examination of the tasks in the table reveals two tasks that show different results with reactivity – the single judgment task used in Fidler (1983) and the multiple, time-critical judgment task used in Dickson et al. (2000).

Different Tasks, Different Results

One task that seems quite simple is the single judgment task used in Fidler (1983), in which participants were asked to predict future grade-point averages (GPAs) in business school for a certain group of undergraduates for whom they had a number of pieces of quantitative information (GMAT scores, college GPA, etc.). In other words, participants had to make a single judgment about each student (future GPA). Results of a within-subjects design showed that verbalization did not affect the participants' decision outcomes, and thus verbalization was non-reactive for task accuracy. By contrast, a more complex judgment task, the forest fire-fighting simulator used in Dickson et al. (2000), required participants to make time-critical, dynamic decisions as the reality of the fire in the simulation changed in response to their actions. In this study, participants were trained on how to use Fire Chief, a computerized forest fire-fighting simulator and then played the role of a fire chief and attempted to control a forest fire by deploying various types of fire-fighting equipment, while verbalizing. In this study, verbalization was found to be reactive. This comparison highlights the differences in the two types of decision-making tasks, one that was simple and involved one decision (Fidler, 1983, which found non-reactivity) and one that was complex, time-critical, and involved multiple decisions in rapid succession (Dickson et al., 2000, which found reactivity). Therefore, it seems that if there are many factors involved in the decision-making process, verbalization can interfere with normal processing, creating reactivity when compared to a silent control group.

Summary

This close examination of tasks used in non-SLA studies reveals a number of trends. First, in their seminal work on verbalization, Ericsson and Simon (1993) indicate that task features interact with verbalization to create reactivity (or non-reactivity). They then suggest that if the justifications and/or explanations that arise from verbalization would normally be produced in the process of solving the task, verbalization should not have any effect on task accuracy (should not be reactive). It stands to reason, then, that if in the process of completing a given task, participants tend to verbalize subvocally, verbalization would be non-reactive. In addition, based on the comparisons of task features in this section, some trends emerge with regard to reactivity. These are summarized in Table 2.14.

From the studies that used the Tower of Hanoi problem and the sugar production/personal interaction simulations, we can infer that greater cognitive demand and the number of factors to consider in order to solve the problem are likely to have led to reactivity. In the CPL tasks, we can infer that task complexity seems to have played a role in reactivity, with a finding of non-reactivity holding true for a simple task but not for a more complex and time-sensitive one. From the studies using simple mathematical operations, we can infer once again that the increased cognitive demand of mental addition (and potentially the demands on working memory) as opposed to subtraction with the aid of pencil and paper combined to result in reactivity. Finally, a comparison of the single judgment (prediction) task and the forest fire-fighting simulator re-iterates that complex tasks

Table 2.14 Comparison of Tasks and Conclusions

Tasks Compared	Conclusion (Reactivity Caused by)
Tower of Hanoi (TOH)	• TOH is cognitively demanding • many factors involved in solution
Sugar production and personal interaction simulators	• task is cognitively demanding • many factors involved in solution
CPL tasks	• task complexity
Raven's Matrices	• no statistical analyses
Subtraction vs. mental addition	• cognitive (attentional) demand caused by mental addition
Single judgment task vs. forest fire-fighting simulator	• complex, multiple judgments • time-critical task in fire-fighting

involving multiple factors and multiple judgments are susceptible to reactivity, as are time-critical tasks.

But how do these task features transfer to SLA? How can this information inform what kinds of tasks are likely to show reactivity in SLA? Chapter 3 describes the nine studies to date that have investigated reactivity in the L2 literature and presents a meta-analysis of those studies, as well as those involving verbal tasks in the non-SLA literature, to help answer that question.

3 Features that Make a Task Amenable to Think-Aloud

A Meta-Analysis of Studies Investigating the Validity of Think-Alouds on Verbal Tasks

Whereas the previous chapter reviewed studies that have investigated the validity of think-alouds in fields other than language acquisition (largely with non-verbal tasks), this chapter focuses on those studies that have been conducted with L2 learners while they engaged in L2 tasks. The nine L2 studies are reviewed in chronological order below.

Reactivity Studies in SLA

Leow and Morgan-Short (2004)

Leow and Morgan-Short (2004) was the first SLA study to empirically investigate the reactivity of think-alouds. The study investigated the effects of non-metacognitive think-alouds on 77 beginning Spanish learners' text comprehension, intake, and written production of formal imperative morphology in Spanish. Learners in the control condition read and completed the tasks silently, while learners in the experimental condition read and completed the tasks while thinking aloud. Results showed non-reactivity, since the two groups did not differ significantly on either text comprehension or post-task assessments of the targeted inflectional morphology. Time on task was not a dependent variable measured in the study, so the issue of latency could not be addressed.

Bowles and Leow (2005)

Expanding on Leow and Morgan-Short (2004), Bowles and Leow (2005) sought to investigate the reactivity of both metacognitive and non-metacognitive think-alouds on text comprehension and item and system learning of the pluperfect subjunctive. Participants were 45 fifth-semester Spanish learners who were randomly assigned to either a control or to one of two verbalization groups (non-metacognitive or metacognitive). All participants read a text that included tokens of the targeted structure and then completed the same comprehension and written production tasks. The only difference between the groups were verbalization instructions; participants in the control group were silent, while those in the non-metacognitive group were instructed to "say whatever passed through [their] minds," and those in the metacognitive group were instructed to comment specifically about their reasoning. Similar to Leow and Morgan-Short (2004), results indicated that, compared to a control group, non-metacognitive verbalization did not significantly affect either comprehension or written production of the targeted form. However, metacognitive verbalization caused a significant decrement in text comprehension but no significant difference for production when compared to either the control or to the non-metacognitive group. Results also indicated that both verbalization groups took significantly more time to read the text and complete the post-assessment tasks than the control group, but that there was no significant difference between the two think-aloud groups in terms of latency.

Sachs and Polio (2007)

Sachs and Polio (2007) examined the reactivity of think-alouds on an L2 writing task. The study was carried out in two experiments. In Experiment 1, 15 adult English as a second language (ESL) learners participated in a three-stage composition–comparison–revision task. Each learner participated in the three-stage process three times, one week receiving written corrections on their compositions, one week receiving reformulations of their errors, and one week receiving reformulations of their errors and verbalizing while they compared their original composition to the reformulated version. Results of a Wilcoxon-signed rank test indicated that when learners were silent during the comparison stage (reformulation), they revised more errors in their composition than when they verbalized during the comparison stage (reformulation + think-aloud), although the effect size ($\eta^2 = .28$) was weak, suggesting that the difference in performance between the two groups, though statistically significant, was small. Experiment 2 was then conducted as a non-repeated-measures study, this time with 54 ESL learners, who were randomly assigned to one of four conditions – (1) error correction, (2) reformulation, (3) reformulation + think-aloud, or (4) control (no feedback). A Mann–Whitney test revealed no significant differences

($p = .77$) between the reformulation and reformulation + think-aloud conditions, indicating that in this second experiment, learners who verbalized during the comparison stage and those who did not corrected a similar number of errors during the revision stage. In summary, verbalization was found to be reactive in Experiment 1, since it appeared to hinder learners' ability to make subsequent revisions to their compositions. In Experiment 2, however, verbalization was found to be non-reactive. In both experiments, learners were instructed to verbalize in English (their L2), unlike in the previous SLA studies (Bowles & Leow, 2005; Leow & Morgan-Short, 2004), which gave learners the option to speak in either their L1 or L2. This difference between Sachs and Polio (2007) and previous studies, combined with the repeated-measures nature of Experiment 1, and the fact that there was not just a single target form is cause for the results to be interpreted with caution.

Sachs and Suh (2007)

Sachs and Suh (2007) investigated the issue of reactivity of think-alouds in the context of synchronous computer-mediated communication (CMC). Thirty ESL learners participated in the study, which targeted sequence of tense in English. All learners interacted individually with the researcher via CMC, first taking a written text completion and interactive story-retelling pre-test, followed by a story-retelling task either with or without textually-enhanced recasts, and with or without the requirement to think aloud. Each learner then completed an interactive story-retelling post-test and a text completion post-test. Learners were allowed to speak in either their L1 (Korean) or in their L2 (English) while thinking aloud, as they preferred. Results indicated that the plus (+) and minus (–) think-aloud groups did not differ significantly in the amount of time spent on task, $t(28) = -.113$, $p = .91$, indicating that verbalization was non-reactive for latency, in contrast to the findings of Bowles and Leow (2005), the one previous SLA study that had examined latency as a dependent variable at that time. Repeated-measures ANOVAs were then run with ± think-aloud as the between-subjects factor, time as the within-subjects factor, and text completion and production (story retelling) as the dependent variables. There was a significant between-group main effect on text completion, $F(1,26) = 6.478$, $p = .02$, which indicates that the group that verbalized performed differently on the text completion test than the group that did not verbalize, regardless of time. No significant interaction effect between time and group was found for either the story retelling or the text completion test, leading the authors to conclude that strong conclusions regarding reactivity should not be drawn from the data.

Rossomondo (2007)

In a study investigating the role of lexical temporal indicators, such as temporal adverbs, in the incidental acquisition of the Spanish future tense, Rossomondo (2007) compared groups of first-semester Spanish students who read a passage silently and those who read the same passage while thinking aloud non-metacognitively. Following recommendations from Ericsson and Simon (1993) and from previous SLA studies, Rossomondo gave participants a sample think-aloud as well as a short warm-up text during which they were instructed to think aloud. After reading the experimental passage, all participants completed a 13-item multiple-choice comprehension test in English, followed by either a 13-item form-recognition task, or a 13-item form-production task. The form-recognition task consisted of 13 target sentences taken from the passage (presented without lexical temporal markers) with a blank where the inflected verb should have been. Participants had to choose the correct inflected form (the future) from among four options. The form-production task consisted of the same 13 target sentences taken directly from the text, but in this case each blank was followed by the infinitive form of a verb in parenthesis, and participants were instructed to conjugate the verb in the same form as in the passage. No reaction time or time on task data was collected, so latency of the think-alouds was not addressed. Results indicated that participants who thought aloud while reading the passage scored statistically similarly on comprehension measures to participants who read the passage silently, $F(1,159) = .078, p = .781$. For recognition and production of the target form, results were quite different, with participants who thought aloud scoring significantly higher on both the form-recognition, $F(1,77) = 12.194, p < .001$, and form-production, $F(1,80) = 7.352, p < .008$, tests.

Bowles (2008)

Bowles (2008) investigated the effects of completing non-metacognitive and metacognitive think-alouds while performing an L2 problem-solving task on subsequent written production of previously encountered and new exemplars of a target form, *gustar*-type psych verbs with dative subjects in Spanish. One hundred and ninety-four first-semester learners of Spanish were randomly assigned to one of six experimental conditions, which differed in terms of type of verbalization (metacognitive, non-metacognitive, or silent) and type of feedback (implicit or explicit). Learners were instructed to speak in either L1 (English) or L2 (Spanish), as they felt most comfortable. Results showed that metacognitive verbalization significantly increased time on task, $F(2, 193) = 15.763$, $p < .0001$, with the metacognitive think-aloud group taking significantly more time to complete the task than either the non-metacognitive or silent group. Metacognitive verbalization also hindered participants' ability to produce exemplars of the target structure on the post-test that they had seen during the experimental task, $F(2,193) = 3.778$, $p < .05$. However, neither type of verbalization significantly affected participants' ability to produce novel exemplars of the target structure, $F(2,193) = 1.713$, $p = .183$ and there was no interaction between verbalization and feedback. These results as a whole indicate that non-metacognitive verbalization was non-reactive for both item and system learning, in accordance with the predictions of Ericsson and Simon's model. However, the results indicate that metacognitive verbalization was reactive on item learning but non-reactive on system learning.

Yoshida (2008)

Yoshida (2008) further investigated the role that verbalization plays in an L2 reading task, thereby building on the work of Leow and Morgan-Short (2004) and Bowles and Leow (2005). In her study, 64 Japanese ESL students were randomly assigned to a verbalization condition (think-aloud or non-think-aloud) and to one of three reading conditions (a control passage, the same passage with questions embedded throughout, or the passage with guidance to help students produce an outline). Students were allowed to think aloud in their L1 (Japanese) or L2 (English) so that their verbalizations would not be constrained by their language ability. The instructions required students to produce metacognitive think-alouds, since they were asked to explain how they made each decision provided in their responses to written while-reading tasks. After reading the passage and completing a corresponding while-reading task, each learner completed a written recall of the propositions in the passage. The recall scores were taken as an indication of reading comprehension, and results of a two-way ANOVA found no significant main effect for reading condition, $F(1,58) = .795$, $p = .376$, or for task type, $F(2,58) = .392$, $p = .677$, and no significant interaction between reading condition and task type, $F(2,58) = .182$, $p = .834$. These results indicate that learners who verbalized performed similarly to learners who did not verbalize, regardless of the task they engaged in while reading. In terms of latency, a two-way ANOVA revealed that the think-aloud group took considerably more time on task than the non-think-aloud group, $F(1,58) = 12.76, p = .001$.

Sanz et al. (2009)

Sanz et al. (2009) reported on two studies that investigated the reactivity of concurrent verbal reports in an L2 instructional lesson. In Experiment 1, 24 L1 English-speaking students, 11 in the think-aloud group and 13 in a silent group, completed a computerized lesson on the Latin case system. After the lesson, participants took an aural interpretation test, a written grammaticality judgment test (GJT), and a sentence production test that required them to drag and drop appropriate morphemes to create a sentence describing an on-screen photograph. On all tests, there was a main effect only for time, indicating that students in both the silent and think-aloud groups learned as a result of the lesson, and that verbalizing during the lesson had neither a facilitative nor a detrimental effect on performance. Sanz et al. (2009) used a more precise measurement than that used in previous studies to measure latency. Whereas previous studies measured total time on task, Sanz et al. (2009) measured mean reaction times on correct responses from the three pre- and post-tests and calculated a grand mean on which to base their overall latency score for each participant. The think-aloud group had longer reaction times than the silent group on just one of the post-tests, the grammaticality judgment, indicating mixed results for latency in this experiment.

In Experiment 2, 24 different college-age students, 11 in the think-aloud group and 13 in the silent group, completed a less explicit version of the treatment used in Experiment 1. The only difference between the two instructional treatments was that treatment in Experiment 1 included an explicit grammar lesson on the case system, whereas the second treatment did not. Instead, students had to rely on knowledge they gained from task-essential practice and explicit feedback. All pre- and post-test measures were the same as in Experiment 1. As in the first experiment, there were main effects for time for all tests, indicating that the treatment caused students to improve in their ability to interpret and produce sentences in Latin. But, in contrast to Experiment 1, there were also reactivity effects because students in the think-aloud group performed significantly better than those in the silent group on both the grammaticality judgment and production tests. In this case, verbalization had a facilitative effect on subsequent performance. As for latency, there were no significant differences in reaction times for the two groups across the three tests, indicating that in this experiment, although verbalization enhanced performance, it did not cause any change in the speed with which participants responded to stimuli in the L2.

Polio and Wang (in review)

Finally, Polio and Wang (in review) replicated Leow and Morgan-Short (2004), with more advanced learners, hypothesizing that the reading strategies of advanced learners might be different enough from those of the beginning learners in the original study to affect reactivity. In Polio and Wang (in review), 30 Chinese L1 learners of English were randomly assigned to a think-aloud or to a silent reading group and were instructed to read a passage in English that was seeded with both frequent and infrequent phrasal verbs. They were instructed to think aloud in English or Chinese, as they felt most comfortable. Upon completing the reading task, participants took a comprehension test (in the L2, English) as well as written production and recognition tests targeting the phrasal verbs found in the passage. Since there were 15 participants per group, less powerful non-parametric statistical tests (Mann–Whitney U tests) were used to compare the performance of the think-aloud and silent groups on the three measures. The only significant difference occurred in comprehension, where participants in the think-aloud group comprehended the text significantly worse than participants in the silent group ($p=.01$). Polio and Wang then examined the contents of the think-alouds to investigate the nature of the reading process for this group of learners. They determined that whereas in Leow and Morgan-Short (2004) translation was the predominant reading strategy, for these advanced learners who used English for academic purposes, translation was relatively uncommon. The researchers hypothesize that this difference in strategy use may have been largely responsible for the differing findings between the original and the replication. Since learners in Leow and Morgan-Short (2004) relied heavily on translation, they were easily able to verbalize the contents of their short-term memory without any effect on comprehension. On the other hand, the learners in the replication were engaging in other, more complex strategies, so it may have been more cognitively demanding for them to verbalize, contributing to the finding of reactivity in comprehension. For the readers' convenience, summaries of the research designs and findings of the SLA studies of reactivity appear in Table 3.1.

Table 3.1 Studies of Reactivity in SLA

Study	Participants	Task(s)	Groups	Design	Reactivity	Non-Reactivity
Leow & Morgan-Short (2004)[a]	77 beginning L2 Spanish learners	Reading	1. Silent control 2. Non-meta TA	Between-subjects	–	1. Text comprehension 2. Recognition and production of target morphology
Bowles & Leow (2005)	45 intermediate L2 Spanish learners	Reading	1. Silent control 2. Non-meta TA 3. Meta TA	Between-subjects	1. Latency (for both TA groups) 2. Text comprehension (for meta TA group)	1. Text comprehension (for non-meta TA group) 2. Production of targeted morphology (both TA groups)
Sachs & Polio (2007) Experiment 1	15 intermediate L2 English learners	Three-stage writing and revision task	1. Error correction (silent) 2. Reformulation (silent) 3. Reformulation + non-meta TA	Within-subjects	1. Number of errors corrected in revised essay	–
Sachs & Polio (2007) Experiment 2	54 intermediate L2 English learners	Three-stage writing and revision task	1. Error correction (silent) 2. Reformulation (silent) 3. Reformulation + non-meta TA 4. No feedback on writing (silent)	Between-subjects	–	1. Number of errors corrected in revised essay
Sachs & Suh (2007)	30 L2 English learners	CMC story-retelling task	1. Silent control 2. Non-meta TA	Between-subjects	1. Text completion post-test	1. Latency 2. Production post-test

Study	Participants	Task	Groups	Design	Measure	Measure
Rossomondo (2007)[a]	6–12 beginning L2 Spanish learners[a]	Reading	1. Silent control 2. Non-meta TA	Between-subjects	1. Form recognition post-test 2. Form production post-test	1. Text comprehension
Bowles (2008)	194 beginning L2 Spanish learners	L2 problem-solving	1. Silent control 2. Non-meta TA 3. Meta TA	Between-subjects	1. Latency 2. Item learning (for meta TA group)	1. System learning (for both TA groups)
Yoshida (2008)	64 intermediate L2 English learners	Reading	1. Silent control 2. Meta TA	Between-subjects	1. Latency	1. Recall (text comprehension)
Sanz, Lin, Lado, Bowden, & Stafford (2009) Experiment 1	24 beginning L2 Latin learners	Instructional lesson w/ explicit pre-task information	1. Silent control 2. Meta TA	Between-subjects	1. Latency (on grammaticality judgment test)	1. Latency (on aural interpretation and sentence production post-tests) 2. Post-test accuracy (on all tests)
Sanz, Lin, Lado, Bowden, & Stafford (2009) Experiment 2	24 beginning L2 Latin learners	Instructional lesson without explicit pre-task information	1. Silent control 2. Meta TA	Between-subjects	1. Post-test accuracy (on aural interpretation test only)	1. Post-test accuracy (on grammaticality judgment test and sentence production tests) 2. Latency
Polio & Wang (in review)[a]	30 advanced L2 English learners	Reading	1. Silent control 2. Non-meta TA	Between-subjects	1. Text comprehension	1. Written production and recognition of targeted structure

Notes
a Indicates time was not measured or reported.
b In Rossomondo (2007), only a small number of participants completed think-alouds for each of the tests (comprehension, $n = 12$, recognition, $n = 6$, production, $n = 6$).

Synthesizing Research on Reactivity

As the reviews of literature in psychology (in Chapter 2) and in SLA (in the previous section) show, there is a mounting body of primary research investigating the reactivity of think-alouds on both verbal and non-verbal tasks. However, no one study on reactivity, regardless of its size, complexity, or number of participants, can provide reliable answers, since individual study findings are susceptible to chance variability and any number of idiosyncrasies in design and sampling. Knowledge about any area is reliably gained through secondary research, which is generally gathered through (1) a narrative review, (2) a vote-counting approach to research review, or (3) a quantitative research synthesis, also referred to as meta-analysis (Light & Pillemer, 1984).

Narrative reviews, such as the one presented in Chapter 2 of the non-SLA literature on reactivity and in the previous section on the SLA literature on reactivity, are helpful in building a picture of the state of research in a given field, but they do not always provide an accurate and cohesive view for a variety of reasons. Different authors may inconsistently sample the primary research on a topic, thereby drawing different conclusions about a single research domain. Even when researchers examine the same body of primary literature, their own beliefs and opinions may lead them to interpret findings differently, or to reconcile contradictory findings in different ways. Perhaps most importantly, researchers conducting a narrative review often base their conclusions on the conclusions drawn by the primary researchers, which in some cases may be flawed, or may be based on too liberal an interpretation of the research data (Dubin & Taveggia, 1968; R. Rosenthal, 1991).

One alternative to a strict narrative review is a vote-counting approach. In a vote-counting review, all primary research studies addressing a given research question are identified and based on the statistically significant (or non-significant) findings, each study is tallied as providing evidence either for or against a given hypothesis. Once all primary studies' "votes" are in, the number of studies with findings supporting or contradicting the hypothesis is tallied, and conclusions are drawn based on the majority finding. Although the procedure for sampling the primary research literature is more comprehensive with the vote-counting approach, there are still drawbacks to this method. Most importantly, the vote-counting method relies on probability values, or the statistical significance or non-significance of each individual study's findings, in order to make conclusions. This method is problematic, given that probability values are highly dependent on sample sizes, with larger sample sizes being more likely to give statistically significant results than smaller sample sizes. In fact, with all other data being equal, two studies observing the same effect may come to opposite conclusions, with one achieving statistically significant differences between groups and the other not finding statistically significant differences, on the basis of sample size alone.

Furthermore, statistical significance conveys only that differences between groups were likely the result of chance at some pre-determined level. An alpha level of .05, for instance, indicates simply that the results obtained could have resulted from chance on just five out of 100 occasions. The probability value does not convey any information about the magnitude of the difference observed between groups; it merely indicates how likely it is that the results were the product of chance. Thus, a very low probability value could be obtained even with a minuscule difference between groups. Light and Pillemer (1984) sum up these facts, stating, "even if every one of 30 studies in a review reports findings that are statistically significant, a vote count does not tell us whether they are large enough to matter in practice" (p. 75). That is, neither narrative nor vote-counting reviews take into account calculations of effect size, or magnitude of difference between groups.

Quantitative meta-analysis is one method of research synthesis that addresses the aforementioned limitations of both the narrative and vote-counting review methods. First, in a meta-analysis, researchers must follow (and report in detail) the principles used to sample the primary literature, and are typically as inclusive as possible in identifying primary studies that have investigated a common research question. Therefore, the sampling procedure is replicable and the synthesis can be built upon by other researchers once further studies have been conducted. Once primary studies have been identified and coded according to a set of substantive and methodological features, descriptive statistics from each unique sample study are used to gauge the effect size of a given treatment or group. There are several different formulas for the calculation of effect size, but one of the most commonly used in social science research is the standardized mean difference, which is the mean difference between an experimental and a control group, with standard deviations and sample sizes taken into account.

Effect sizes of individual studies can be averaged to determine a mean effect size, summarizing the effectiveness of a given treatment across studies, or they can be compared to provide insight into variables that could have caused differing findings between two studies.

Effect sizes have the advantage of not being dependent on sample size, or on probability values. Furthermore, quantitative meta-analyses take into account how frequent and consistent the observed effects are across studies by providing calculations of standard error and confidence intervals.

Meta-Analysis

The remainder of this chapter presents the results of a meta-analysis of research on the reactivity of think-alouds used in conjunction with verbal tasks. As the narrative review of studies on reactivity of think-alouds shows, the majority of studies have used non-verbal tasks, such as the Tower of Hanoi, or the Katona card problem, to investigate the issue of reactivity. This meta-analysis is focused on a subset of tasks, from the fields of both psychology and SLA, which have investigated the reactivity of concurrent verbal reports on *verbal* tasks.

Meta-analyses are often used in one of two capacities – as exploratory tools in a developing field of inquiry or as confirmatory instruments in better-developed fields with a larger research base (J. M. Norris & Ortega, 2000). Despite the fact that think-alouds have been used in SLA research for many years, because investigations into their reactivity are in their infancy, an exploratory meta-analysis is appropriate in this case.

Besides providing a summary of existing research in different fields, a meta-analysis compares the outcomes of a range of studies with an array of independent variables, in an attempt to identify patterns. In SLA, meta-analyses have increased in frequency in the past decade, as researchers in the field have started to adopt the method to provide more comprehensive answers to long-standing questions, such as the role of instruction in SLA (J. M. Norris & Ortega, 2000), the efficacy of different types of corrective feedback (Russell & Spada, 2006), the effects of conversational interaction (Keck et al., 2006; Mackey & Goo, 2007), the impact of attitude and motivation (Masgoret & Gardner, 2003), and visual/textual input enhancement (Lee & Huang, 2008) on language learning.

The main research question that this meta-analysis seeks to answer is: "Are think-alouds reactive for accuracy and/or latency when used in conjunction with verbal tasks?" In that regard, it seeks to provide more comprehensive answers to the controversy surrounding the use of think-alouds in language research. Within that broadly defined question there are several sub-questions:

1. What is the role of the following factors in causing reactivity?

   a. Type of verbal report (non-metacognitive vs. metacognitive).
   b. Language of verbal report (L1 vs. L2 vs. combination of L1 and L2).
   c. Language of task (L1 vs. L2).
   d. Type of task (reading vs. writing vs. grammar learning vs. meta-language).
   e. L2 proficiency (beginning vs. intermediate vs. advanced).

2. What is the effect of thinking aloud on the following dependent measures?

   a. Text comprehension (receptive vs. productive).
   b. Form learning (receptive vs. productive).
   c. Latency (time on task vs. reaction times).

Identification of Studies

Since reactivity studies involving verbal tasks have been conducted both in psychology and in linguistics, I searched the PsycInfo database, in addition to Linguistics and Language Behavior Abstracts (LLBA) and the Education Resources Information Center (ERIC) databases to identify studies for the meta-analysis. Since verbal reports have been used so widely, particularly in cognitive psychology, an initial search in the three databases with the keyword "verbal report(s)" returned more than 1,500 results, far too many to reliably check. I therefore narrowed the search, using the following terms to search the subjects, abstracts, and keywords, and combinations thereof: "concurrent verbal report(s)," "concurrent verbal protocol(s)," "reactivity," "think-aloud(s)," "verbal task," and "language task." Then, using the same set of subject and keywords, I replicated the search in major SLA journals to ensure that published studies had not been missed. For this, I conducted separate searches in each of the following journals: *Applied Linguistics, Applied Psycholinguistics, Canadian Modern Language Review, Computer Assisted Language Learning, Foreign Language Annals, International Journal of Educational Research, Language Learning, Language Learning & Technology, Language Teaching Research, The Modern Language Journal, ReCALL, Second Language Research, Studies in Second Language Acquisition, System, and TESOL Quarterly.* Subsequently, I also visited the websites of the journals to review the lists of articles in press, to determine whether there were any relevant studies accepted, but not yet in print, at the time of writing. In one case, a relevant paper on reactivity was listed as being in press at the time of writing, so I contacted the authors of the paper to obtain it for inclusion in the meta-analysis (Sanz et al., 2009).

Following recommendations in the SLA literature (J. M. Norris & Ortega, 2006), unpublished papers, sometimes referred to as the "fugitive literature" (M. C. Rosenthal, 1994) were included in the meta-analysis to the extent possible. As authors of previous meta-analyses have discussed (Mackey & Goo, 2007; J. M. Norris & Ortega, 2006), there are advantages and disadvantages both to including and excluding such unpublished studies. In an effort to be as inclusive as possible, using the methods described in Rosenthal (1994) and through personal contact with researchers working in the area of reactivity, one unpublished empirical study on reactivity was identified for inclusion in the meta-analysis. (At the time of writing, the study was being reviewed for publication, but an editorial decision had not yet been made.)

Selection Criteria

The studies identified through the subject, abstract, and keyword searches were narrowed down by using the following selection criteria.

INCLUSION CRITERIA

1. The study was published, in press, or drafted (in the case of fugitive studies) prior to February 2009.
2. The study compared one or more verbalization groups to a silent (control) group, or it compared one or more verbalization groups to each other, in the absence of a silent (control) group.
3. At least one of the verbalization groups required participants to verbalize concurrently, while performing some type of verbal task that had as its main purpose either language comprehension or production.
4. Participants in the studies could be either adults or children. It is important to note that children in all of the studies were verbalizing (and completing verbal tasks) in their L1. To disentangle the two variables, language of verbalization and language of the task were coded separately for each study.
5. The study included sufficient descriptive statistics to enable the calculation of effect sizes. (Three studies – Rhenius and Deffner (1990), Russo et al. (1989), and Stratman and Hamp-Lyons (1994) – were excluded from the meta-analysis on this basis.)[1]

6. The study included sufficient information to be coded according to the coding scheme adopted.
7. Studies written in English, French, and German all appeared as results in the database searches and were evaluated for inclusion. That is, no study was excluded simply on the basis of language of publication.

EXCLUSION CRITERIA

1. Studies were excluded from the analysis if concurrent verbalization, although a part of the study design, was not an independent variable (Piolat & Olive, 2000; Witte & Cherry, 1994).

Coding

Since this meta-analysis is exploratory in nature, being the first of its kind in either the psychological or the SLA literatures, a broad range of categories were coded for each study. Following previous SLA meta-analyses (Mackey & Goo, 2007; J. M. Norris & Ortega, 2006), the effects of both substantive and methodological features were examined. Substantive features are those that are theoretically-motivated as playing an influential role in a study's outcome, whereas methodological features are those related to context that might also play a role in the outcomes.

A total of 14 unique sample studies, described in 12 research reports, were identified for inclusion in the meta-analysis. Those are listed in Appendix A and categorized according to their substantive and methodological features in Appendix B.

In terms of substantive features, each study was coded based on features of the verbal reports used, the tasks participants performed while verbalizing, and the dependent variables used to gauge performance. Instructions given to participants in think-aloud conditions were examined carefully, and each study was subsequently coded according to the language participants were allowed to use in the think-aloud (L1, L2, or a combination of L1 and L2). Verbalization instructions were also examined to determine the type of report used in each study (silent/control, non-metacognitive, or metacognitive). Next, features of the verbal tasks that participants performed while thinking aloud were identified. First, each task was coded according to whether it was in the L1 or L2 of the participants. Then, each task was categorized according to type (reading, writing, grammar learning, or meta-language). The category "meta-language" was used to describe tasks that required participants to treat language as an object, such as anagrams and analogies. Finally, all studies were coded according to the dependent variables used. Since several of the studies involved reading tasks, it was deemed necessary to code the measures of text comprehension in detail. All text comprehension measures were coded as either receptive (e.g. multiple-choice questions based on a reading passage) or productive (which was further categorized as either free constructed, in which participants were asked to respond to some sort of prompt or to provide a recall, or constrained constructed, in which participants were asked simply to fill in a blank.) All assessments used to measure grammatical form learning were coded according to the same categories as the text comprehension assessments. Finally, for the studies that measured and reported latency, the dependent variable was either time on task or reaction time.

Additionally, a series of methodological features having to do with learner characteristics were also coded. First, each study was coded according to the total number of participants and number of participants per cell. Then, participants were placed into one of three categories (beginning, intermediate, or advanced) based on their reported proficiency level in the L2. Following Lee and Huang (2008), proficiency was coded according to the four-way classification distinction proposed in Thomas (2006): (a) impressionistic judgment, (b) institutional status, (c) in-house assessment, or (d) standardized test(s). Finally, participants in each study were coded according to the amount of knowledge of the targeted form(s) they displayed at the outset of the study (no formal exposure/demonstrated knowledge or partial knowledge.)

Calculation of Effect Sizes

Two families of effect size measures are commonly used in quantitative meta-analysis, the *r* family and the *d* family (R. Rosenthal, 1991). Cohen's *d*, from the *d* family, was chosen for this meta-analysis, since it has been used widely in other meta-analyses in SLA (Keck et al., 2006; Mackey & Goo, 2007; J. M. Norris & Ortega, 2000) and since it can be computed using relatively few pieces of descriptive statistical information. Given the means, standard deviations, and sample sizes of the treatment and control groups in an experimental study, Cohen's *d* can be easily calculated using Formula 3.1:

$$d = \frac{\bar{x}_T - \bar{x}_C}{S}, \text{ where } S \text{ is the pooled standard deviation.} \qquad (3.1)$$

The Cohen's *d* statistic is simple to interpret, with $.2 \leq d \leq .5$ indicating a small effect size, $.5 \leq d \leq .8$ indicating a medium effect size, and $d \geq .8$ indicating a large effect size (J. Cohen, 1988).

For small sample sizes, where the degrees of freedom are 50 or less, it is necessary to apply a correction factor to the resulting d value. Following Hedges et al. (1989), the correction factor J was obtained through Formula 3.2 and multiplied by d to create an unbiased d value corrected for small n size:

$$J = 1 - \frac{3}{4(n_c - n_t - 2) - 1} \tag{3.2}$$

In all except three cases, discussed below, means and standard deviations were used to calculate Cohen's d effect sizes, which were then corrected as needed on the basis of sample size.

For three studies included in the meta-analysis (Mathews et al., 1989; Sachs & Polio, 2007; Short et al., 1991), means and standard deviations were not provided. Nevertheless, the results of inferential statistical tests were provided in enough detail to enable the calculation of effect size estimates through more indirect means, as described below.

In Mathews et al. (1989) and Short et al. (1991), ANOVAs or F tests were used, and both the F statistic and the mean sum of squares were reported. For those two studies, Cohen's d was calculated using the F value and the sample size, as shown in Formula 3.3:

$$d = \sqrt{\frac{F}{n}} \tag{3.3}$$

In Sachs and Polio (2007), proportions of revised T-units per essay were provided. Following Cooper and Hedges (1994) and Mackey and Goo (2007), Cohen's h estimates of effect size were calculated in this case, since their values are interpreted on the same scale as Cohen's d values. Cohen's h is the difference between the proportions in the treatment and control groups, after each has been transformed to radians in an arcsine transformation. Specifically, Cohen's h was computed using Formula 3.4, from Cooper and Hedges (1994, p. 235):

$$h = 2(\arcsin \sqrt{proportion_T}) - 2(\arcsin \sqrt{proportion_C}) \tag{3.4}$$

Combining Effect Sizes

Some meta-analysts believe that each unique study sample should contribute just one effect size to a meta-analysis (Light & Pillemer, 1984). In cases where multiple treatments are carried out in a single sample study, then, effect sizes are combined across the range of treatments. In this meta-analysis, it was decided that each study could contribute more than one effect size, on the theoretical grounds that an identical sample of participants may perform differently while verbalizing, depending on a number of factors, including the type of task (Russo et al., 1989). Since several of the studies examined participants' performance on a range of tasks, and with a range of dependent measures, to combine them all into one effect size would have blurred many possible distinctions that could have come to light as a result of the meta-analysis. Therefore, all of the effect sizes calculated for each unique sample study are reported in Appendix B, and the relevant effect size estimates for each research question are included in a step-wise fashion.

In order to answer the research questions of interest, it was necessary to combine effect sizes from several studies. Although there are various methods for combining effect sizes, the method chosen for this meta-analysis was to form a weighted average, weighting each effect size estimate by the reciprocal of its sampling variance, (i.e. the reciprocal of its squared standard error). Hedges et al. (1989) refer to this weighting method as "the statistically optimal way to average a group of independent estimates" (p. 46) because it takes into account the sample sizes and sampling errors of each study, rather than treating all studies with their various *n* sizes equally. Specifically, the formula used to calculate a weighted average appears in Formula 3.5:

Where $d_1, d_2, d_3 \ldots d_k$ are k independent effect size estimates with standard errors $S_1, S_2, S_3 \ldots S_k$, the weighted average effect size is

$$d_t = \frac{\dfrac{d_1}{S_1^2} + \dfrac{d_2}{S_2^2} + \dfrac{d_3}{S_3^2}}{\dfrac{1}{S_1^2} + \dfrac{1}{S_2^2} + \dfrac{1}{S_3^2}} \tag{3.5}$$

The formula to calculate the standard error of that weighted average appears in Formula 3.6:

$$S_{d_t} = \frac{1}{\sqrt{\dfrac{1}{S_1^2} + \dfrac{1}{S_2^2} + \dfrac{1}{S_K^2}}} \tag{3.6}$$

Analysis of the Homogeneity of Effect Sizes

Effect sizes from various studies should be combined only when the meta-analyst has good reason to believe that the studies are similar, at least on several dimensions, substantive and/or methodological. Even then, it is essential to quantitatively analyze the studies in terms of both their individual effect sizes and variances. The appropriate test, known as a homogeneity test, determines whether the variability across effect sizes is greater than or less than what would be expected from sampling error alone. The most commonly used homogeneity test in meta-analysis is a Q test. If the Q value is less than the critical value of a χ^2 test with the same number of degrees of freedom, then the group of studies is homogenous.

> [T]his result tells us that the effect sizes do not differ by more than would be expected from sampling error and, hence, are virtual replications in their findings. Even though the studies may differ on a variety of characteristics, methodological and substantive, none of those differences matter in terms of the magnitude of the effects found by the studies.
> (Lipsey & Wilson, 2001, p. 162)

The formula for calculating the Q statistic is given in Formula 3.7 below (from Lipsey & Wilson, 2001):

Where, for each study,
w = inverse variance weight, wes = effect size (ES) * w, and $wessq$ = ES^2 * w

$$Q = \sum wessq - \frac{(\sum wes)^2}{\sum w} \qquad (3.7)$$

In cases where a group of studies is found to be homogenous, "the mean effect size is clearly a representative and meaningful summary of the distribution of effect size values" (Lipsey & Wilson, 2001, p. 162).

Sometimes even when studies have been grouped by substantive and methodological variables and are considered to be similar enough to warrant averaging their effect sizes, the Q statistic resulting from the homogeneity test is greater than the critical value of a χ^2 with the relevant number of degrees of freedom. In those cases, the studies are said to be heterogeneous, and the variability observed is larger than what would be due to different samples across the different studies.

> When studies that presumably examine the same thing disagree, it is neither wise nor especially meaningful to resolve their differences simply by averaging them all together. The average over contrary results is not likely to converge on the truth, just muddle it.
> (Lipsey & Wilson, 2001, p. 162).

In such cases, further analysis is needed to determine if there is some other principled reason to believe that the studies have divergent effect sizes. At this point, the meta-analyst returns to the coding sheet to examine the studies' characteristics. As described in detail in Lipsey and Wilson (2001), there are several quantitative approaches to dealing with heterogeneity and determining its source. The present meta-analysis operates from the assumption that a portion of the excess variance can be modeled with variables that have been coded in the coding sheet. Lipsey and Wilson (2001) recommend conducting an analog to the ANOVA in order to test the ability of a categorical variable, such as task type or type of report, to explain the excess effect size variability. Complete instructions for carrying out the analog to the ANOVA either with spreadsheets or with statistical packages are provided in Lipsey and Wilson (2001). Essentially, though, the procedure determines how much of the total variability can be explained by the categorical variable in question.

Results

The 14 unique sample studies were coded and examined according to the established coding categories, summarized below, to provide a comprehensive overview of the characteristics of the studies included in the meta-analysis.

Publication Characteristics

Nine of the 12 reports (75 per cent) were published in refereed journals in either SLA or psychology. Specifically, five of the reports were published in *Studies in Second Language Acquisition*, and one each was published in *Language Learning, Memory and Cognition, Journal of Experimental Psychology: Learning, Memory, and Cognition*, and *Contemporary Educational Psychology*. Three of the twelve reports (25 per cent) were published in edited volumes (Bowles et al., 2008; Mackey, 2007; Schmid & Zambarbieri, 1991), and one study was, at the time of writing, being submitted for publication to a journal, and as such was not counted in the tallies. Figure 3.1 shows the number of empirical studies included in this meta-analysis according to year of publication. As the graph clearly shows, there has been increased interest in the reactivity of think-alouds in recent years, with eight of the studies published since 2007.

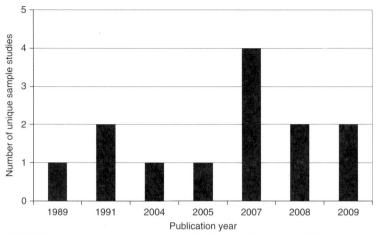

NOTE: Thirteen unique sample studies are included in this graph. The fourteenth (Polio & Wang, in review) is included in the meta-analysis but not in the graph since no publication decision had been reached at the time of writing.

Figure 3.1 Empirical Studies Included in the Meta-Analysis According to Year of Publication

Learner Characteristics

A total of 1,023 participants were involved in the 14 unique sample studies. As shown in Table 3.1, there was a wide range of n sizes across the studies, with a minimum of 15 and a maximum of 194 participants in a single study. Across studies, the mean number of participants was 73.07, and the median was 54.5. (Silent) control groups tended to have slightly larger numbers of participants than their experimental (think-aloud) counterparts (Table 3.2).

Eleven of the 14 studies (78 per cent) came from the field of SLA and had participants who were learning a second/foreign language. Participants in all of the studies were enrolled in either Spanish (4/11) or English (5/11) classes, with the exception of the learners in the two experiments reported in Sanz et al. (2009), who were monolingual English-speakers being taught a small amount of Latin as part of the study. Language proficiency information for the learners in the 11 SLA studies is provided in Table 3.3.

As the information in Table 3.3, represented graphically in Figure 3.2, shows, learners were drawn mainly from the lower levels of language proficiency, with 9 out of 11 studies (82 per cent) including

Table 3.2 Sample Size Across Studies and Groups

Measure	Full Study	Experimental Group	Control Group
Mean	73.07	38.50	42.36
SD	59.95	35.93	39.62
Median	54.50	24.50	25.00
Maximum	194	125	140
Minimum	15	11	11
Range	179	114	129
Total	1,023	539	593

beginning and intermediate-level learners. Just one study included exclusively advanced-level (ESL) students in its design.

Researchers assessed the proficiency of their participants in a variety of ways, as exemplified in Figure 3.3. The most commonly used method of determining proficiency was institutional status (37 per

Table 3.3 Language and Proficiency Level of Participants in Each Sample Study

Unique Sample Study	Language of Study	Proficiency	How Proficiency Defined
Bowles (2008)	Spanish	Beginning	Institutional status
Leow and Morgan-Short (2004)	Spanish	Beginning	Institutional status
Bowles and Leow (2005)	Spanish	Intermediate	Institutional status
Sachs and Suh (2007)	English	Intermediate	n.r.
Sachs and Polio (2007) Experiment 1	English	Intermediate	In-house placement
Sachs and Polio (2007) Experiment 2[a]	English	n.r.	n.r.
Yoshida (2008)	English	Intermediate	Standardized test
Sanz, Lin, Lado, Bowden, & Stafford (2009) Experiment 1	Latin	Beginning	Background questionnaire
Sanz, Lin, Lado, Bowden, & Stafford (2009) Experiment 2	Latin	Beginning	Background questionnaire
Rossomondo (2007)	Spanish	Beginning	Institutional status
Polio & Wang (in review)	English	Advanced	Standardized test

Notes
n.r. = not reported.
a Learners were described only as being from a "variety of levels."

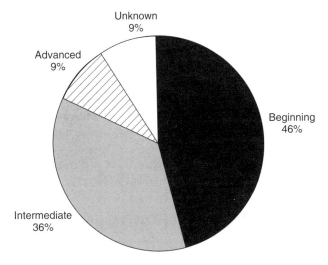

Figure 3.2 Language Proficiency of Learners in SLA Reactivity Studies

cent), indicating that in these studies the participants' progression through the institution's language course sequence was taken to be an indicator of their overall language proficiency. This appears to be the rule, rather than the exception, in SLA studies, given that previous research has also found institutional status to be the most commonly used predictor of proficiency (Keck et al., 2006; Mackey &

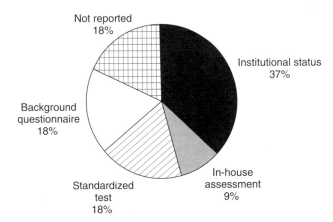

Figure 3.3 Method Used to Determine Language Proficiency in SLA Studies on Reactivity

Goo, 2007; Thomas, 2006). The studies in the sample also frequently used standardized tests, such as the TOEFL, to measure proficiency (18 per cent) or asked learners to report their exposure/proficiency in the language on a background questionnaire (18 per cent).[2] However, an equal percentage of studies (18 per cent) did not report how language proficiency was assessed, leaving the readers to wonder if the learners in the sample truly formed a homogeneous group. Just a small percentage (9 per cent) used an in-house, locally developed language assessment to determine learners' proficiency.

Effect sizes for each independent variable will be discussed below and are compiled in Table 3.4 for readers' reference.

Effects of Type of Report on Post-Test Performance

To determine the effect that type of report (non-metacognitive vs. metacognitive) had on task performance as compared to a silent control group, studies were divided by type of report and then by post-test measure (text comprehension vs. tests of receptive form learning vs. tests of productive form learning vs. latency). The mean effect sizes for type of report on post-test performance are discussed below and represented graphically in Figure 3.4.

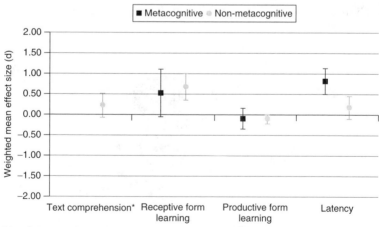

*Note: Only one study (Bowles & Leow, 2005) examined the effect of metacognitive verbalization on text comprehension. Therefore, there were insufficient data points to compute a weighted mean effect size for that measure and consequently there is no representation of it on the figure.

Figure 3.4 Effect of Type of Report on Post-Test Performance

Table 3.4 Reactivity Effect Sizes

Independent Variable	N	Weighted Mean D	95% CI Lower	Upper
Type of Report				
Text Comprehension				
Metacognitive[a]	1	n.a.	n.a.	n.a.
Non-metacognitive[b]	4	0.21	−0.07	0.50
Form Learning (Receptive)				
Metacognitive	2	0.51	−0.07	1.09
Non-metacognitive[c]	4	0.67	0.34	1.00
Form Learning (Productive)				
Metacognitive[d]	7	−0.11	−0.36	0.15
Non-metacognitive[e]	10	−0.12	−0.24	−0.02
Latency				
Metacognitive	7	0.80	0.49	1.12
Non-metacognitive[f]	4	0.17	−0.11	0.45
Language of Verbal Report				
Text Comprehension				
L1	—	n.a.	n.a.	n.a.
L2	—	n.a.	n.a.	n.a.
L1/L2	6	0.04	−0.23	0.32
Form Learning (Receptive)				
L1	—	n.a.	n.a.	n.a.
L2	—	n.a.	n.a.	n.a.
L1/L2	4	0.27	−0.04	0.59
Form Learning (Productive)				
L1[g]	2	0.36	0.09	0.63
L2	2	−0.14	−0.26	−0.01
L1/L2	16	−0.07	−0.23	0.07
Latency				
L1	—	n.a.	n.a.	n.a.
L2	—	n.a.	n.a.	n.a.
L1/L2[h] metacognitive	6	0.82	0.47	1.16
non-metacognitive	3	0.25	−0.09	0.59
Language of Task				
Text Comprehension				
L1	—	n.a.	n.a.	n.a.
L2	8	0.01	−0.22	0.25
Form Learning (Receptive)				
L1	—	n.a.	n.a.	n.a.
L2	7	0.47	0.21	0.74
Form Learning (Productive)				
L1[i]	2	0.11	−0.14	0.35
L2[j] metacognitive	7	−0.11	−0.36	0.15
non-metacognitive	10	−0.10	−0.21	0.01

Latency					
L1		—	n.a.	n.a.	n.a.
L2[k]	metacognitive	7	0.80	0.48	1.11
	non-metacognitive	4	0.16	−0.11	0.44
Type of Task					
Text Comprehension					
Reading		6	0.04	−0.23	0.31
Form Learning (Receptive)					
Reading[l]		3	0.61	0.23	0.97
Writing		—	n.a.	n.a.	n.a.
Grammar learning		2	0.51	−0.07	1.09
Meta-language		—	n.a.	n.a.	n.a.
Form Learning (Productive)					
Reading		6	0.19	−0.09	0.46
Writing		2	−0.14	−0.26	−0.01
Grammar learning[m]	explicit	3	−0.53	−0.86	−0.20
	implicit	4	0.16	−0.05	0.37
Meta-language		—	n.a.	n.a.	n.a.
Latency					
Reading		4	1.16	0.74	1.58
Writing		—	n.a.	n.a.	n.a.
Grammar learning		4	0.25	−0.07	0.58
Meta-language		—	n.a.	n.a.	n.a.

Notes

n.a. = not applicable.

a   Just one study (Bowles & Leow, 2005) measured the text comprehension of participants who thought aloud metacognitively while reading.

b   The original set of five studies violated the assumption of homogeneity of distribution. Further analysis revealed that significant variance could be accounted for by the one study that had learners of advanced L2 proficiency (Polio & Wang, in review). When it was removed, the assumption of homogeneity of distribution was met by the remaining four studies, reported in this row.

c   Again, the original set of five studies violated the assumption of homogeneity of distribution. Further analysis revealed that significant variance could be accounted for by the one study that had learners of advanced L2 proficiency (Polio & Wang, in review). When it was removed, the assumption of homogeneity of distribution was met by the remaining four studies, reported in this row.

d   The seven studies used to calculate the weighted mean effect size are all L2 studies. Including L1 studies caused the distribution of effect sizes to be heterogeneous.

e   When all 11 studies were included, the assumption of homogeneity of distribution was violated. Rossomondo (2007) was subsequently removed because of its unusually high variance, and the resulting ten studies produced the weighted effect size reported in this row.

f   The original set of five studies violated the assumption of homogeneity of distribution. Further analysis revealed that significant variance could be accounted for by the one L1 study. When it was removed, the assumption of homogeneity of distribution was met by the remaining four studies, reported in this row.

g   The original set of three studies violated the assumption of homogeneity of distribution. Further analysis revealed that significant variance could be accounted for by type of report. When the one non-metacognitive study was removed, the assumption of homogeneity of distribution was met by the remaining two (metacognitive) studies, reported in this row.

h   The entire set of nine studies violated the assumption of homogeneity of distribution. Further analysis revealed that significant variance could be accounted for by type of report. When the studies were further separated by type of report, the assumption of homogeneity of distribution was met, so the results reported in this row are separated by type of report (metacognitive vs. non-metacognitive).

i   The original set of three studies violated the assumption of homogeneity of distribution. Further analysis revealed that significant variance could be accounted for by one study (Short, Schatschneider, Cuddy, Evans, Dellick, & Basili, 1991), the only study with child participants. With this study removed, the assumption of homogeneity of distribution was met for the remaining two studies, so the results reported in this row are for just those that had adult participants.

j   The entire set of 17 studies violated the assumption of homogeneity of distribution. Further analysis revealed that significant variance could be accounted for by type of report. When the studies were further separated by type of report, the assumption of homogeneity of distribution was met, so the results reported in this row are separated by type of report (metacognitive vs. non-metacognitive).

k   The entire set of 11 studies violated the assumption of homogeneity of distribution. Further analysis revealed that significant variance could be accounted for by type of report. When the studies were further separated by type of report, the assumption of homogeneity of distribution was met, so the results reported in this row are separated by type of report (metacognitive vs. non-metacognitive).

l   The original set of four studies violated the assumption of homogeneity of distribution. Further analysis revealed that significant variance could be accounted for by the one study that had L2 learners of advanced proficiency (Polio & Wang, in review). Once this study was removed, the assumption of homogeneity of distribution was met for the remaining three studies, the results of which are presented in this row.

m   The original set of seven studies violated the assumption of homogeneity of distribution. Further analysis revealed that significant variance could be accounted for by the degree of explicitness of the grammar task ($\pm$ explicit). When the studies were further separated by explicitness, the assumption of homogeneity of distribution was met, so the results reported in this row are separated by explicitness (explicit vs. implicit).

Effect of Type of Report on Text Comprehension

There was just one study (Bowles & Leow, 2005) that examined the performance of students completing metacognitive think-alouds on text comprehension. Therefore, there were insufficient data to calculate an average effect size for metacognitive verbalization on this measure. It should be noted that although there have been five independent sample studies examining the effect of non-metacognitive think-alouds on text comprehension, the effects of metacognitive think-alouds are understudied to date, and future research should address this gap in the literature.

The assumption of homogeneous distribution was rejected for the five independent sample studies that examined the performance of students completing non-metacognitive think-alouds on text comprehension. The significant Q value obtained for this group of studies ($Q = 11.92$, $df = 4$, $p < .05$) indicates that the variance across this set of studies was greater than what would be expected due to sampling error alone. Another look at the coding sheet revealed that all of the studies except one (Polio & Wang, in review) were conducted with participants at beginning or intermediate levels of L2 proficiency. The group becomes homogeneous when proficiency is taken into account. Removing the one study with advanced learners, a significant effect for proficiency was found, $p < .05$. Although it is important to be cautious in generalizing based on the effect for proficiency, since it was due to just one study, this result highlights an area in need of future research. Once more studies are conducted with learners at the higher end of the proficiency scale, more decisive conclusions will be able to be drawn.

The resulting four studies produced a weighted average effect size of $d = .21$, with a 95 per cent confidence interval ranging from $-.07$ to .50. Since this confidence interval overlaps the zero value, it cannot be said to be statistically reliable, so more research is needed to verify that students who think aloud non-metacognitively while reading have moderately better text comprehension than their counterparts who read without verbalizing.

Effect of Type of Report on Receptive Form Learning

There were two independent sample studies that examined the performance of students completing metacognitive think-alouds on tests of receptive form learning (Sanz et al., 2009, Experiments 1 and 2). The two studies produced a weighted effect size of $d = .51$, with a 95 per cent confidence interval ranging from $-.07$ to 1.09. Since this confidence interval overlaps the zero value, it cannot be said to be statistically reliable, so more research is needed to verify that students who think aloud metacognitively have moderately better receptive form learning than their counterparts who do not verbalize while completing L2 tasks.

The assumption of homogeneous distribution was rejected for the five independent sample studies that examined the performance of students completing non-metacognitive think-alouds on tests of receptive form learning. The significant Q value obtained for this group of studies ($Q = 13.47$, $df = 4$, $p < .05$) indicates that the variance across this set of studies was greater than what would be expected due to sampling error alone. Again, when the one study with learners of advanced proficiency (Polio & Wang, in review) was removed, the remaining set of four studies was homogeneous. The weighted effect size of the four studies was $d = .67$, with a 95 per cent confidence interval ranging from

.34 to 1.00. Since this confidence interval does not overlap the zero value, it is taken to be statistically reliable. In other words, when learners think-aloud non-metacognitively, they perform consistently better on subsequent tests of receptive form learning than do students who complete the same L2 task silently.

Effect of Type of Report on Productive Form Learning

The assumption of homogeneous distribution was rejected for the nine independent sample studies that examined the performance of students completing metacognitive think-alouds on tests of productive form learning. The significant Q value obtained for this group of studies ($Q = 20.52$, $df = 8$, $p < .05$) indicates that the variance across this set of studies was greater than what would be expected due to sampling error alone. When the two studies conducted with L1 tasks were removed, the remaining set of seven studies was homogeneous. This result suggests that the effects of thinking aloud may be different depending on whether the participants are completing tasks in their L1 or in their L2. The weighted effect size of the seven studies was $d = -.11$, with a 95 per cent confidence interval ranging from −.36 to .15. Given that the confidence interval spans across the zero value, the results cannot be said to be statistically reliable. Further research is necessary to determine whether metacognitive verbalization has a slight negative impact on productive form learning in L2 tasks.

Similarly, the assumption of homogeneous distribution was rejected for the 11 independent sample studies that examined the performance of students completing non-metacognitive think-alouds on tests of productive form learning. The significant Q value obtained for this group of studies ($Q = 21.07$, $df = 10$, $p < .05$) indicates that the variance across this set of studies was greater than what would be expected due to sampling error alone. In this case, removing the one L1 study in the group still resulted in a heterogeneous distribution ($Q = 20.51$, $df = 9$, $p < .05$). However, removing the Rossomondo study, which had unusually high variance, resulted in a set of ten studies that was homogeneously distributed, with a weighted effect size of $d = -.12$ and a 95 per cent confidence interval ranging from −.23 to −.02. This result indicates that when learners engaged in either an L1 or L2 verbal task think aloud non-metacognitively, they have decreased productive form learning compared to learners who did not verbalize during the task.

Effect of Type of Report on Latency

The seven studies that measured latency for participants who were thinking aloud metacognitively met the assumption of homogeneity and had a weighted effect size of $d = .80$, with a 95 per cent confidence interval ranging from .49 to 1.12. This result indicates that thinking aloud metacognitively consistently adds to the time on task compared to silent task performance.

The five studies that measured latency for participants who were thinking aloud non-metacognitively did not meet the assumption of homogeneity ($Q = 12.54$, $df = 4$, $p < .05$). When the one L1 study (Lass et al., 1991), the only study with a negative effect size, was removed, the distribution became homogeneous. The weighted effect size of the remaining four studies was $d = .17$, with a 95 per cent confidence interval ranging from −.11 to .45. Because the values overlap the zero mark, it cannot be reliably said that non-metacognitive verbalization consistently adds to time on task.

Effects of Language of Report on Post-Test Performance

The mean effect sizes for language of report (L1, L2, or a combination of the two) on post-test performance are discussed below and represented graphically in Figure 3.5.

Effects of Language of Report on Text Comprehension

All of the studies that had reading tasks and measured reading comprehension were L2 studies. All six of them gave learners the choice to speak in the L1 or L2, or a combination thereof, during the task. Therefore, it is impossible to draw any conclusions about the effect of verbalizing exclusively in the L1 or the L2 on reading comprehension, and future research in this area is warranted. Rossomondo (2007), which also included a reading task, could not be included in this analysis since specific information about the language of verbal report is not given in the report of her study.

The six independent sample studies that measured reading comprehension for learners who had the option to speak in either the L1 or the L2, or a combination thereof met the assumption of homogeneous distribution of effect sizes. The weighted effect size for the six studies was $d = .04$, with a 95 per cent confidence interval ranging from −.23 to .32. This result indicates that when learners were allowed to choose what language to report in, their reading

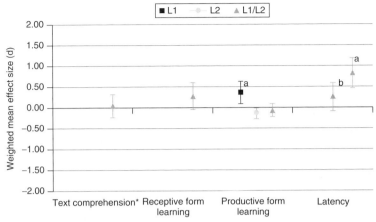

a = Includes metacognitive think-alouds only.
b = Includes non-metacognitive think-alouds only.
*Note: Since most studies allowed participants to think aloud in either the L1, the L2, or a combination thereof, most of the weighted effect sizes were calculated for this combined language of report. There were not enough studies for weighted effect sizes to be calculated for think-alouds produced in just the L1 or just the L2 for text comprehension, receptive form learning, or latency. Consequently, those values are not plotted on the graph.

Figure 3.5 Effect of Language of Report on Post-Test Performance

comprehension scores were only marginally higher than those of their counterparts who did not think aloud while reading. Furthermore, the confidence interval of this value crosses the zero interval, indicating that the results are not statistically reliable, and that more research is needed to verify this finding.

Effects of Language of Report on Receptive Form Learning

Similarly, all of the studies that used receptive measures of form learning were SLA studies. Again, none of those studies required learners to speak entirely in their L1 or entirely in the L2 during the think-aloud. Learners in all four studies were given the option to speak in the L1, in the L2, or a combination of the two. Therefore, no conclusions can be drawn about the effects of verbalizing entirely in the L1 or the L2 on receptive form learning in SLA.

The assumption of homogeneity of distribution was met for the four studies that measured receptive learning, and the weighted effect size was $d = .27$, with a 95 per cent confidence interval ranging from $-.04$ to $.59$.

Effects of Language of Report on Productive Form Learning

There were three studies that required learners to speak in the L1 and used productive measures of form learning. For this set of studies, the assumption of homogeneity of distribution was violated ($Q = 8.20$, $df = 2$, $p < .05$), but type of report (non-metacognitive vs. metacognitive) was found to account for a significant ($p < .05$) amount of between-study variation. The distribution of the two metacognitive studies' effect sizes was found to be homogeneous, resulting in a weighted effect size of $d = .36$, and a 95 per cent confidence interval ranging from .09 to .63. This result indicates that learners who think aloud in the L1 have moderately better productive form learning than learners who complete the tasks silently.

There were just two studies that used productive measures of form learning that required learners to speak in the L2. The studies, which were Experiments 1 and 2 from Sachs and Polio (2007), asked students to provide non-metacognitive reports in their L2 (English) while completing writing tasks. The assumption of homogeneity of distribution was met, and the weighted effect size was $d = -.14$, with a 95 per cent confidence interval ranging from $-.26$ to $-.01$. Given that the confidence interval ranges are all negative, it is possible to conclude that verbalizing in the L2 has a detrimental effect on productive form learning, at least within the confines of these studies, which had multiple, rather than single, linguistic targets and were conducted in the time constraints of a normal classroom period.

The vast majority of studies that included measures of productive form learning ($n = 16$) allowed learners to verbalize in either their L1 or their L2. For this set of studies, the assumption of homogeneity of distribution was met, and the weighted effect size was $d = -.07$, with a 95 per cent confidence interval ranging from $-.23$ to .07. This result suggests that when learners are allowed to choose which language to verbalize in, they perform slightly worse on measures of productive form learning than a silent control group of learners. But given that this interval includes both negative and positive values, the result is not statistically reliable, and more research is needed to verify the finding.

Effects of Language of Report on Latency

None of the studies that required learners to verbalize in either their L1 or their L2 used measures of latency, so it is not possible to determine what effect language of report has on latency. However, there were nine studies that allowed learners to choose whether to verbalize in the L1, L2, or a combination thereof and that measured latency. The assumption of homogeneity of distribution was not met ($Q = 19.13$, $df = 8$, $p < .05$). When type of report (non-metacognitive vs. metacognitive) was taken into account, the distribution became homogeneous, resulting in a set of six metacognitive studies ($d = .82$, 95 per cent confidence interval ranging from .47 to 1.16) and three non-metacognitive studies ($d = .25$, 95 per cent confidence interval ranging from –.09 to .59). These results indicate that when learners verbalize metacognitively and choose the language of report, they require substantially more time to complete the task than a silent control group. When learners verbalize non-metacognitively, the results are less clear, given the relatively small mean effect size and the fact that the confidence interval includes both negative and positive values.

Effects of Language of Task on Post-Test Performance

The mean effect sizes for language of task (L1 or L2) on post-test performance are discussed below and represented graphically in Figure 3.6.

Effects of Language of Task on Text Comprehension

No L1 studies involved reading tasks, so consequently none measured text comprehension. It is therefore impossible to draw conclusions about how verbalization would affect comprehension of a text in a participant's L1.

However, there have been eight studies that have used L2 reading tasks and have measured text comprehension. The assumption of homogeneity of distribution was met for those studies, which had a weighted effect size of $d = .01$ and a 95 per cent confidence interval ranging from –.22 to .25. This result indicates a very small improvement in text comprehension by L2 learners who verbalized while reading, as compared to L2 learners who read silently. But since the confidence interval overlaps zero, this result is not statistically reliable and more investigation is needed.

Effects of Language of Task on Receptive Form Learning

Again, none of the reactivity studies involving L1 tasks have included measures of receptive form learning, so no conclusions about this effect can be drawn. However, seven studies involving L2 tasks have used measures of receptive form learning. For those

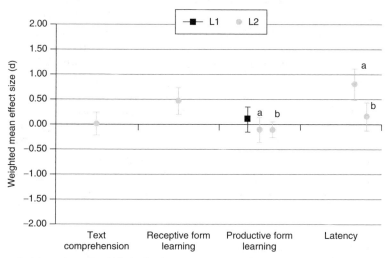

a = Includes metacognitive think-alouds only.
b = Includes non-metacognitive think-alouds only.
*Note: Since most of the reactivity studies have been conducted in SLA, there were fewer tasks conducted in the L1 than in the L2. There were not enough studies for weighted effect sizes to be calculated for think-alouds from L1 studies for text comprehension, receptive form learning, or latency. Consequently, those values are not plotted on the graph.

Figure 3.6 Effect of Language of Task on Post-Test Performance

studies, the assumption of homogeneity of distribution was met, with a weighted effect size of $d = .47$ and a 95 per cent confidence interval ranging from .21 to .74. This result indicates a medium-sized facilitative effect for verbalization on receptive form learning in L2 tasks.

Effects of Language of Task on Productive Form Learning

There are three L1 reactivity studies to date that have measured productive form learning. The assumption of homogeneity of distribution for those studies was violated ($Q = 8.20$, $df = 2$, $p < .05$), but once the single study involving child participants (Short et al., 1991) was removed, the distribution of the remaining two studies was homogeneous, with a weighted effect size of $d = .11$ and a 95 per cent confidence interval ranging from −.14 to .35. This result indicates that when learners verbalize in their L1, they have slightly improved productive form learning compared to learners who did not verbalize while performing the learning task. But since the confidence interval contains both negative and positive values, it is not statistically reliable, indicating that further research is needed.

A total of 17 L2 reactivity studies have used productive measures of form learning. The assumption of homogeneity of distribution was violated for that set ($Q = 32.15$, $df = 16$, $p < .05$), but once the studies were separated by type of report (non-metacognitive vs. metacognitive) the distribution of the two sets became homogeneous. This division resulted in ten non-metacognitive L2 studies of productive form learning, with a weighted effect size of $d = -.10$ and a 95 per cent confidence interval ranging from $-.21$ to $.01$, and seven metacognitive studies with a weighted effect size of $d = -.11$, with a confidence interval ranging from $-.36$ to $.15$. These results suggest that verbalizing while completing an L2 task slightly reduces productive form learning as compared to a group that completed the same L2 task silently. But the 95 per cent confidence intervals for both non-metacognitive and metacognitive reports contain both negative and positive values, indicating that performance can range from slightly decreased form learning to slightly increased form learning. Again, further research is needed.

Effects of Language of Task on Latency

Just one of the L1 reactivity studies (Lass et al., 1991) used measures of latency, so no conclusions can be drawn about whether verbal tasks conducted while thinking aloud in one's native language require more time to complete than the same tasks completed silently. However, 11 L2 reactivity studies used measures of latency. This set of studies violated the assumption of homogeneity of distribution ($Q = 24.54$, $df = 10$, $p < .05$), but separating the studies by type of report (non-metacognitive vs. metacognitive) resulted in two sets with homogeneous distributions. For the four non-metacognitive studies involving L2 tasks, the weighted effect size was $d = .16$, and the 95 per cent confidence interval ranged from $-.11$ to $.44$. This result suggests that overall, when learners verbalize non-metacognitively on an L2 task, they require slightly more time to complete the task than a silent group does. However, the pattern is stronger for the seven metacognitive studies involving L2 tasks, which had a weighted effect size of $d = .80$, with the 95 per cent confidence interval entirely in the positive range, from $.48$ to 1.11. That is, when learners verbalize metacognitively on an L2 task, they require a good deal more time to complete the task than a silent group would.

Effects of Type of Task on Post-Test Performance

Finally, the effects of type of task (reading, writing, grammar learning, or meta-language) on reactivity were investigated. The mean effect sizes for type of task on post-test performance are discussed below and represented graphically in Figure 3.7.

Effects of Type of Task on Text Comprehension

Since the only task type that included a measure of text comprehension was reading, effect sizes were weighted and averaged for the six reading tasks that included text comprehension measures. The studies met the assumption of homogeneity of distribution, and the resulting weighted effect size was $d = .04$, with a 95 per cent confidence interval ranging from $-.23$ to $.31$. This suggests that thinking aloud while reading marginally improves text comprehension as compared to reading silently. However, since the confidence interval contains both negative and positive values, more research is needed to verify the conclusion.

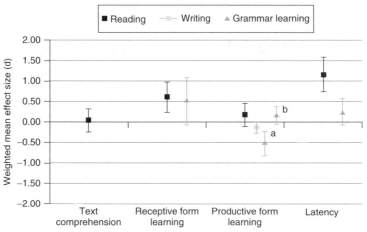

a = Includes studies involving explicit grammer instruction only.
b = Includes studies involving implicit grammer instruction only.
*Note: There were not enough studies for weighted effect sizes to be calculated for think-alouds from meta-language tasks. Similarly, the studies involving writing tasks did not include measures of receptive from learning or latency. Consequently, those values are not plotted on the graph.

Figure 3.7 Effect of Type of Task on Post-Test Performance

Effects of Type of Task on Receptive Form Learning

This meta-analysis revealed four (L2) studies that have used reading tasks and have measured receptive form learning of think-aloud groups compared to silent groups. The assumption of homogeneity of distribution was violated ($Q = 11.44$, $df = 3$, $p < .05$), but once the single study with advanced proficiency L2 learners was removed, the remaining three studies, all of which were conducted with beginning and/or intermediate L2 learners, were shown to have a homogeneous distribution. The weighted effect size was $d = .61$, and the 95 per cent confidence interval ranged from .23 to .97. This result indicates that when L2 learners at beginning and/or intermediate proficiency levels think aloud while reading, they have higher levels of receptive form learning than those who read the text silently. Since there was just one study with advanced learners, it is not possible to determine whether advanced proficiency learners in fact behave differently than beginning/intermediate learners with regard to reactivity, or whether this particular study simply had greater sampling error. This is another area where future research is certainly warranted.

None of the reactivity studies that used writing tasks included any receptive measures of form learning. Instead, the two studies that used writing tasks (Sachs & Polio, 2007, Experiments 1 and 2), used only production measures. Therefore, it was not possible to do any analysis of the relationship between thinking aloud while writing and subsequent receptive form ability.

There were two L2 studies (Sanz et al., 2009, Experiments 1 and 2) that compared the receptive form learning of a think-aloud and a silent group while they completed a grammar learning task. Both instructed learners to provide metacognitive think-alouds, and the assumption of homogeneity of distribution was met. The weighted effect size of the studies was $d = .51$, with the 95 per cent confidence interval ranging from $-.07$ to 1.09. Although the result is not statistically reliable, the medium-sized d value indicates that learners who verbalized (albeit metacognitively) while completing a grammar task performed better on tests of receptive form learning than learners who completed the same task silently. Although no studies to date have addressed the issue, future research should address the role of type of report (non-metacognitive vs. metacognitive) as well.

As was the case with reactivity studies that used writing tasks, the few studies that used meta-language tasks did not measure receptive learning. That is, all of the post-tests required learners to produce forms, so no conclusions can be drawn about the effects of thinking aloud during meta-language tasks on receptive form learning.

Effects of Type of Task on Productive Form Learning

There were six reactivity studies that used reading tasks and measured productive form learning of think-aloud groups compared to silent groups. The distribution of the effect sizes of the studies met the assumption of homogeneity, resulting in a weighted effect size of $d = .19$ and a 95 per cent confidence interval ranging from $-.09$ to .46. This result, although not statistically reliable, indicates that learners who think aloud while reading have slightly higher scores on post-tests that measure language form production than learners who read silently.

There were just two studies that used writing tasks and measured productive form learning of think-aloud groups compared to silent groups. The two studies' effect size distributions met the assumption of homogeneity, resulting in a weighted effect size of $d = -.14$, and a 95 per cent confidence interval ranging from $-.26$ to $-.01$. Since all of the values are in the negative range, the result indicates that thinking aloud while writing has a small, detrimental effect on productive form learning compared to writing silently. It is important to note, however, that both studies asked participants to think-aloud non-metacognitively while writing, so further research is needed to determine if the effect would be the same for metacognitive verbalization.

A total of seven studies compared the productive form learning of think-aloud groups to silent groups engaged in grammar learning tasks. The assumption of homogeneity of distribution was violated for this set of studies ($Q = 17.87$, $df = 9$, $p < .05$). Explicitness of the grammar learning task was found to account for a significant portion of the variation, and when the studies were separated in this way, their distributions were homogeneous. The resulting explicit grammar learning studies ($n = 3$) had a weighted effect size of $d = -.53$, and a 95 per cent confidence interval ranging from $-.86$ to $-.20$. This indicates that thinking aloud while performing an explicit grammar learning task hinders learners' subsequent productive form ability as compared to a group who performed the task silently. The implicit grammar learning studies ($n = 4$) showed a different pattern of results, with a weighted effect size of $d = .16$ and a 95 per cent confidence interval ranging from $-.05$ to .37. This result indicates that thinking aloud while performing an implicit grammar learning task slightly facilitated learners' subsequent productive form ability as compared to a group who performed the task silently. However, since the confidence interval around this weighted effect size overlaps the zero value, its results cannot be taken as statistically reliable, necessitating further research in the area.

A total of two (L1) studies compared the productive form learning of think-aloud groups compared to silent groups engaged in meta-language tasks. The assumption of homogeneity was not met for the pair of studies ($Q = 7.87$, $df = 1$, $p < .05$), probably due to the nature of the participants in the studies. (One contained adult participants and the other contained child participants.) Separating the studies into groups resulted in just one study per group, making it impossible to conduct any further analysis.

Effects of Type of Task on Latency

A total of four studies compared the latency of think-aloud groups compared to silent groups engaged in reading tasks. The assumption of homogeneity was met, and the resulting weighted effect size was $d = 1.16$, with a 95 per cent confidence interval ranging from .74 to 1.58. This large effect size shows that when learners are engaged in reading tasks, thinking aloud requires much more time than reading silently.

Neither of the studies that compared think-aloud groups to silent groups engaged in writing tasks (Sachs & Polio, 2007, Experiments 1 and 2) measured time on task. Therefore, it is not possible to determine whether thinking aloud while writing increases time on task, as it does for reading tasks.

A total of four studies compared the latency of think-aloud groups compared to silent groups engaged in grammar learning tasks. The distribution of effect sizes was homogeneous, resulting in a weighted effect size of $d = .25$ and a 95 per cent confidence interval ranging from $-.07$ to .58. This result suggests that thinking aloud does not require as much additional time on grammar learning tasks as it does on reading tasks.

Only one study that had participants engage in a meta-language task (Lass et al., 1991) provided measures of time on task. Therefore, no combination of effect sizes or further analysis was possible.

Effects of L2 Proficiency on Post-Test Performance

All but one SLA study on reactivity to date (Polio & Wang, in review) has included beginning and/or intermediate-level L2 learners. Therefore, there is insufficient data to analyze the effect of proficiency on reactivity of think-alouds at this time. Given that significant between-study variance was accounted for by language proficiency when receptive form learning was measured (1) for learners completing reading tasks and (2) for learners providing non-metacognitive reports, it should be taken as an important variable in future reactivity research.

Discussion

The main research question that this meta-analysis seeks to answer is: "Are think-alouds reactive for accuracy and/or latency when used in conjunction with verbal tasks?" It was not possible to average the effect sizes of all studies to produce grand weighted mean ds for accuracy or for latency because the distributions violated the assumption of homogeneity. This result indicates that the answer to the question of reactivity and think-alouds is not a simple "yes" or "no" but rather is dependent on a host of variables.

By way of summary, however, effect sizes were generally $d \leq .5$ for all measures of accuracy, indicating that there is a small difference in performance when a think-aloud group is compared to a group that completes the same verbal task silently. However, the effect sizes indicate that thinking aloud does generally require substantially more time than silent task completion, with effect sizes for latency ranging as high as $d = 1.16$ when participants are required to think aloud while reading.

A response to each of the sub-parts of each research question is provided below, followed by a summary of major findings.

RQ 1a: What is the role of type of verbal report (non-metacognitive vs. metacognitive) in causing reactivity?
For accuracy, effect sizes for type of verbal report were small to medium, ranging from $d = -.12$ to .67. Specifically, non-metacognitive verbalization had a small, facilitative effect ($d = .21$) on comprehension compared to a silent control group. Metacognitive and non-metacognitive verbalization had small, detrimental effects on measures of productive form learning ($d = -.11$ and $-.12$, respectively). Medium effect sizes were only observed on measures of receptive form learning, where the weighted mean effect size was $d = .51$ for metacognitive verbalization and $d = .67$ for non-metacognitive verbalization.

As for latency, the pattern of findings regarding type of report is clearer. The weighted mean effect size of $d = .8$ indicates that metacognitive reports significantly increase time on task compared to silent task completion. Time on task is only slightly increased (d = .17) for non-metacognitive reports.

RQ 1b: What is the role of language of verbal report (L1 vs. L2 vs. combination of L1 and L2) in causing reactivity?
Most of the studies that have examined the reactivity of think-alouds on verbal tasks have allowed learners to think aloud in their L1, L2, or a combination thereof. On all measures of accuracy, effect sizes were small, ranging from −.07 to .27. Since there were just two studies each that investigated the effect of thinking aloud in the L1 or in the L2 on reactivity, more research is needed to determine what happens when learners are not free to choose the language in which they verbalize. In terms of latency, the distribution of effect sizes was not homogeneous, even for the studies in which learners chose the language of verbalization. But type of report accounted for significant between-study variance, with a weighted mean of d = .82 for metacognitive reports and d = .25 for non-metacognitive reports. That is, when allowed to verbalize in the language of their choice, learners require a large amount more time to produce metacognitive reports than to complete the task silently. To produce non-metacognitive reports, learners require a small amount more time than to complete the task silently.

RQ 1c: What is the role of language of task (L1 vs. L2) in causing reactivity?
A broader array of studies on reactivity has been conducted with L2 tasks than with L1 tasks, making few comparisons regarding language of task possible. The existing L1 studies, which included only measures of productive form learning, produced a small weighted mean effect size of d = .11, with the 95 per cent confidence interval overlapping zero, indicating that either a small negative or positive effect for thinking aloud is possible. The weighted mean effect size for L2 studies on measures of productive form learning was small (d = −.11). Since its 95 per cent confidence interval also overlaps zero, it is understood that regardless of whether the verbal task is in a participant's L1 or L2, think-alouds seem to have a small effect on productive form learning compared to a silent control group.

No L1 studies on reactivity have measured latency. For the L2 studies that have included measures of time on task and reaction times, there was a heterogeneous distribution of effect sizes. The between-study variance was accounted for by type of report, with metacognitive think-alouds having a mean effect size of $d = .80$ and non-metacognitive think-alouds a small effect size of $d = .16$. Again, metacognitive think-alouds require substantially more time to complete than non-metacognitive think-alouds, and both require more time than silent task completion.

RQ 1d: What is the role of type of task (reading vs. writing vs. grammar learning vs. meta-language) in causing reactivity?
To date, the most commonly investigated task type in reactivity studies is reading. This is not surprising, since the first SLA reactivity study (Leow & Morgan-Short, 2004) examined the effects of think-alouds on L2 reading. With reading tasks, think-alouds had a small, positive effect on both text comprehension ($d = .04$) and productive form learning ($d = .19$). However, the facilitative effects were medium in size for receptive form learning ($d = .61$).

With writing tasks, there have been few reactivity studies. A small, negative effect size ($d = -.14$) was found for think-alouds on tests of productive form learning. Since the confidence interval for this effect size is entirely in the negative range, the result indicates that thinking aloud while writing has a detrimental effect on productive measures of form learning.

There have also been just a few reactivity studies involving grammar learning tasks, with a medium-sized, positive effect ($d = .51$) on receptive tests of form learning. On tests of productive form learning, however, all of the grammar learning studies could not be grouped together because the assumption of homogeneous distribution was violated. The between-study variance was explained by a difference in the grammar learning conditions, with think-alouds having a medium-sized detrimental effect on productive form learning ($d = -.53$) when the grammar learning task involved explicit instruction and a small, facilitative effect ($d = .16$) when the grammar learning task involved implicit instruction.

Since there have been just two studies of reactivity involving meta-language tasks, and since their distribution was not homogeneous, analysis of this task type was not possible.

Latency measures were taken only on reading and grammar learning tasks. In both cases, thinking aloud increased time on task, but for grammar learning, the effect size was small ($d = .25$), whereas for reading tasks, the effect size was large ($d = 1.16$), indicating that thinking aloud slows reading substantially, and to a greater extent than in grammar learning tasks.

RQ 1e: What is the role of L2 proficiency (beginning vs. intermediate vs. advanced) in causing reactivity?

Since all of the L2 reactivity studies except one (Polio & Wang, in review) were conducted with either beginning or intermediate proficiency L2 learners, an in-depth analysis of the effect of proficiency was not possible. However, the fact that the study with advanced proficiency learners was an outlier among non-metacognitive think-aloud studies on text comprehension and receptive form learning, and among reading studies on receptive form learning, suggests that proficiency is a variable that should be taken into account and studied systematically. It also highlights the fact that existing studies can make generalizations only about the effects of thinking aloud on lower proficiency level L2 learners' task performance.

RQ 1f: What is the effect of thinking aloud on text comprehension?

Abstracting across the independent variables just discussed, thinking aloud has a small, facilitative effect on text comprehension, ranging from $d = .01$ to .21.

RQ 1g: What is the effect of thinking aloud on form learning (receptive vs. productive)?

On measures of receptive form learning, thinking aloud has a small to medium-sized, facilitative effect, ranging from $d = .27$ to .67. Similarly, on measures of productive form learning, thinking aloud has a medium-sized effect, although it ranges from being detrimental ($d = -.53$) to being facilitative ($d = .36$).

RQ 1h: What is the effect of thinking aloud on latency (time on task vs. reaction times)?

Just two unique sample studies included in this meta-analysis (Sanz et al., 2009, Experiments 1 and 2) used reaction times to measure latency. All of the remaining studies used coarser measures such as total time on task. But despite the measurement tool that was used, across all of the independent variables, thinking aloud was shown to slow down task completion. The range, however, is broad, extending from $d = .16$ on the low end, to $d = 1.16$ on the high end. Such a range suggests that while thinking aloud will cause time on task to increase, the effect may be small, as it was for grammar learning tasks or quite large, as it was for reading tasks.

Summary of Major Findings

In summary, the major finding of this meta-analysis is that thinking aloud while completing a verbal task has a small effect on post-task performance. In other words, compared to participants completing the same tasks silently, participants who think aloud tend to perform only slightly better or slightly worse on post-tests. The results for time on task are more decisive, indicating across the board that thinking aloud increases time on task. Nevertheless, effect sizes for latency ranged from small (d = .16) to very large (d = 1.16), with the largest effects demonstrated when participants were required to think aloud while performing reading tasks.

Perhaps even more importantly, it was not possible to average the effect sizes of all studies to produce grand weighted mean ds for accuracy or for latency because those effect size distributions violated the assumption of homogeneity. This result indicates that the answer to the question of reactivity and think-alouds is not a simple "yes" or "no" but rather is dependent on a host of variables. Subsequent analyses to identify the sources of between-study variance revealed that some variance could be attributed to expected sources, such as type of report (metacognitive vs. non-metacognitive), which has been discussed at length in the psychology literature (Ericsson & Simon, 1993). In other cases, the sources of between-study variance that were identified may be unique to the language research context. Most notably, the variables of L2 proficiency level and explicitness of instruction, previously under-studied as independent variables in reactivity research, were found to account for significant between-study variance. Research is most desperately needed to determine the role that these factors play in determining whether think-alouds will or will not be reactive.

Areas in Need of Future Research

The systematic coding and analysis of reactivity studies has revealed several areas that, despite their theoretical importance, have been under-investigated. At the same time, this meta-analysis has high-lighted the role that several previously untested variables, such as L2 proficiency, may have on whether thinking aloud is or is not reactive.

A look at Table 3.4, which displays the weighted mean effect sizes for each of the independent variables, reveals several areas in which there were few (or no) studies. Lacking are studies that examine the effect of using just one language (either L1 or L2) in thinking aloud. This is because most of the studies conducted so far have examined the reactive effects of think-alouds when participants were allowed to select either the L1 or the L2, or to use a combination of the two languages, in their reports. Certainly, this is a gap in the research that should be filled.

Similarly, some task types have been investigated more heavily than others with regard to reactivity. Topping the list are studies that have examined the reactivity of think-alouds on reading ($n = 6$) and grammar learning tasks ($n = 7$). But the effect of think-alouds on the writing process has only been investigated in two unique sample studies, making it untenable to draw firm conclusions about reactivity with this task type.

More research is clearly needed overall in examining reactivity in conjunction with verbal tasks, given the paucity of reactivity research with language tasks as compared to non-verbal and problem-solving tasks. Empirical studies are needed to test the sources of between-study variance identified in this meta-analysis to determine to what extent they affect reactivity. L2 proficiency and explicitness of instruction are paramount among them.

4 Data Collection Considerations

Whereas Chapters 1 and 2 traced the history of think-alouds in cognitive psychology and SLA, and Chapter 3 provided a quantitative meta-analysis of studies using think-alouds in conjunction with verbal tasks, this chapter is more practical in nature. Specifically, this chapter is designed to assist any researcher who is considering using think-alouds.

Instructions for Research Participants

Informed Consent

Prior to participating in the study, as part of the informed consent process, research participants should receive explicit written explanation of the think-aloud procedure. This explanation should not be technical in nature, but rather written in plain language. Minimally, the informed consent document should specify that participants' voices will be audio-recorded and that no personally identifiable information will be stored or published along with the speech samples or transcripts thereof. That is, the participants' anonymity is maintained, even in cases where excerpts of think-alouds are published as part of an academic presentation or paper. And, although it is not expressly required, many Institutional Review Boards or ethics committees recommend that the researcher explain to the participants what will be done with their voice samples. Clearly, the goal is not to give away the study (Mackey & Gass, 2005). Nevertheless, it is possible to provide general information about how the participants' think-alouds will contribute to the field of language research. The example below, taken from the informed consent document for Bowles and Leow (2005), demonstrates how such wording can be general and yet informative to research participants:

If you agree to participate in this study, you will be asked to complete Spanish language tasks on two separate occasions. In part 1, you will do a written exercise that should take approximately 10–15 minutes to complete. In part 2, you will read a text in Spanish and answer some questions about it. While you are reading the text, you will be asked to think your thoughts out loud and your voice will be audiotaped. These recordings will help us to better understand how students read in a second language.

Think-Aloud Instructions

Once research participants have consented to participate and to have their voices audio-recorded, they should not merely be instructed to speak their thoughts out loud. Rather, a formal protocol that has been designed (and preferably pilot-tested) in advance is necessary. The protocol should, minimally, (1) reiterate the reason the participants are being asked to think aloud, (2) provide instructions about how they should think aloud, and (3) include a warm-up task during which participants practice thinking aloud and have time to ask the researchers any questions about the process before beginning the operational study.

Re-iterate the Reason for Thinking Aloud

Typically, the first sentence or two of the think-aloud instructions reiterates why the participants are being asked to think aloud (Bowles, 2008; Bowles & Leow, 2005; Ericsson & Simon, 1984, 1993; Leow & Morgan-Short, 2004; Rosa & Leow, 2004a, 2004b; Rosa & O'Neill, 1999). This statement should be general, as the example below from Bowles (2008) shows: "In this experiment I am interested in what you think about when you complete these tasks. In order to find out, I am going to ask you to THINK ALOUD as you work through the mazes."

The researcher could choose to provide more information about the ultimate use of the think-alouds, or the contribution that they will make to the research base. For instance, a researcher investigating L2 reading might begin the think-aloud instructions with: "This experiment is designed to investigate how second-language learners process texts they read in their second language. For this reason, I would like to know what you are thinking as you read the following text." Any brief description will do, as long as it clearly and accurately represents the use of the think-alouds and does not give away the goal of the study. For example, if the researcher working on L2 reading were investigating vocabulary learning through glossing, it would be inappropriate for the think-aloud instructions to contain information that would lead the participants to conclude that special attention would be paid to glossed words, or to unknown vocabulary in the text.

Provide Instructions about How to Think-Aloud

Immediately following the rationale for having participants think-aloud, the verbalization instructions should detail specifically what the researcher intends the participants to do. Minimally, this set of instructions should include (1) a description of what is meant by "thinking aloud," (2) the language(s) participants are allowed to use to verbalize their thoughts, and (3) the level of detail and reflection required in the think-aloud. An excerpt of the think-aloud instructions used in Sanz et al. (2009, p. 53) exemplifies these features:

> [W]e ask you to TALK ALOUD as you go through the program. What we mean by "talk aloud" is that we want you to say out loud everything that you would say to yourself silently while you think. Just act as if you were alone in the room speaking to yourself. Don't try to explain your thoughts.

Sanz et al. (2009) do not mention the language(s) that participants are allowed to use in the think-alouds because their learners were monolingual native English speakers who were being exposed to Latin for the first time through the computerized lesson that formed part of the study. Therefore, it was assumed that their think-alouds could only be completed in English, possibly with occasional references to the Latin words included in the lesson. With any other participant group, however, including relatively low proficiency language learners, it is essential to specify which language(s) are acceptable to use. Learners, particularly those who are accustomed to communicative language classrooms, may assume that they are to speak their thoughts aloud in the second language, if they are not otherwise instructed. Additionally, not specifying the language(s) of verbalization introduces variability into the research design of the study and creates a situation in which some participants may think aloud entirely in the L1, while others may force themselves to think aloud entirely in the second language and might therefore be unable to communicate some of their thoughts as effectively as they could in the L1. To date, all but one SLA study (Sachs & Polio, 2007) has allowed learners to think-aloud in their L1 and/or L2, as they felt most comfortable. Since there is little empirical evidence about the effects of thinking aloud in the L1 vs. the L2, researchers should be cautious about requiring participants to verbalize entirely in the L2.

As the excerpt from Sanz et al. (2009) shows, verbalization instructions should also explain what type of think-aloud is expected. Participants need not be instructed to provide *non-metacognitive* or *metacognitive* think-alouds per se; such technical terminology is likely to be confusing. Rather, the instructions from Sanz et al. (2009, p. 53) clearly and simply demonstrate the level of detail that participants are expected to provide when thinking aloud, in this case non-metacognitively:

> What we mean by "talk aloud" is that we want you to say out loud everything that you would say to yourself silently while you think. Just act as if you were alone in the room speaking to yourself. Don't try to explain your thoughts.

Sanz et al. (2009) did not have a metacognitive think-aloud condition, but an excerpt from the verbalization instructions used in Bowles (2008, p. 386) shows how a similar explanation can be given for learners in metacognitive think-aloud conditions:

> As you go through the maze, give a reason for choosing each path. Give a justification out loud for choosing each path and explain what you are thinking. Please provide as thorough a justification as possible, as if you were explaining to someone learning Spanish why you are choosing the paths you choose.

If at all possible, it is advisable to pilot-test the verbalization instructions (as well as all other task materials) on a small number of participants whose data will not be included in the final sample. Pilot-testing helps to ensure that the verbalization instructions are written clearly, in a way that participants understand and can follow. Any ambiguities that are found during pilot-testing can be corrected prior to the operational study. (For many other reasons to conduct pilot studies, see Mackey and Gass, 2005.)

As a case in point, in the pilot study leading up to Bowles (2008), participants were scrolling past the on-screen verbalization instructions and beginning the warm-up task without reading them. The problem was remedied in the operational study by setting a timer on the screen that presented the verbalization instructions so that participants could not move on to the next screen until one minute had elapsed.

Warm-Up Task

Continuing the tradition begun in cognitive psychology with Ericsson and Simon's (1984, 1993) books on verbalization, it is customary to provide participants with a warm-up task during which they think-aloud, thereby familiarizing themselves with the process and ensuring that they understand the verbalization instructions. Studies in cognitive psychology most commonly have participants "practice" thinking aloud by doing an arithmetic problem and verbalizing while carrying out the computation. Some SLA studies have reported using arithmetic problems as warm-ups (Bowles & Leow, 2005; Leow & Morgan-Short, 2004; Sanz et al., 2009), whereas others (Bowles, 2008) have used short verbal problems as the warm-up task. Each has advantages and disadvantages. With arithmetic problems, participants are practicing on a non-verbal task in preparation to carry out a verbal task, so it may be more difficult for them to extrapolate from thinking aloud in this type of practice to the operational study. However, one advantage to using an arithmetic problem is that since it is non-verbal, the practice itself does not, as Sanz et al. (2009) point out, "put words in participants' mouths" (p. 67). Verbal warm-up tasks, on the other hand, have the advantage that they are more similar to the operational tasks, so learners may be able to go from the practice verbalization to the operational study more easily. However, any verbal warm-up should be carefully chosen so that it does not prime the participants for the target structure being investigated in the study. Whichever option the researcher chooses, it is important that participants have a warm-up task during which they can think aloud and ask any questions about the procedure before the experiment begins.

Preparing participants to verbalize is just one of the considerations that must be taken into account when using think-alouds, however. In the following sections, other considerations, such as the type of language task being used, the type and language of verbalization, and time constraints will be discussed.

Type of Language Task

As mentioned in Chapter 3, think-alouds may not be appropriate to use in conjunction with all types of language tasks. Clearly, any oral task would not be compatible with concurrent think-alouds. Researchers using oral tasks would be better served by retrospective stimulated recalls, discussed at length in Gass and Mackey (2000).

Think-alouds have been used in a variety of other task types, including reading (Leow & Morgan-Short, 2004; Polio & Wang, in review; Rossomondo, 2007; Yoshida, 2008), writing (Sachs & Polio, 2007), written computer-mediated interaction (Sachs & Suh, 2007), and self-paced grammar modules (Sanz et al., 2009). It should be noted, however, that although the results of the quantitative meta-analysis presented in Chapter 3 are based on a small body of existing empirical studies, reactivity was more commonly found with reading tasks than with the other task types investigated to date. As the meta-analysis also suggests, a host of factors is likely responsible for this result, but researchers should take appropriate caution when using think-alouds in conjunction with reading tasks.

Since participants are believed to be able to verbalize only a portion of their explicit, rather than implicit, knowledge, researchers should assume that the contents of think-alouds represent explicit language knowledge. Ellis (2004) has suggested that think-alouds can be used to provide insight into "what kinds of explicit knowledge learners exploit and in what ways" (p. 268). In fact, Ellis (2004) indicates that think-alouds should be used as a complement to language tests to tap explicit knowledge, given that "another entirely different approach based on tasks that elicit verbal reports is also needed" (p. 268).

In some cases, a researcher may decide to have participants think aloud during language assessment measures, as in Leow and Morgan-Short (2004), Bowles and Leow (2005), and Bowles (2008). Given that participants are thought to have a limited ability to verbalize implicit knowledge, it is advisable to use think-alouds only during language assessments designed to tap explicit knowledge. Therefore, think-alouds would seem to be appropriate to use in conjunction with untimed GJTs, metalinguistic knowledge tests (Ellis, 2005), and any other type of assessment designed to elicit explicit knowledge, such as tests of controlled written production. Conversely, think-alouds would be *inappropriate* to use in conjunction with timed GJTs (Ellis, 2005), or with any other test designed to tap implicit language knowledge.

Type and Language of Verbalization

The decision about whether to require participants to think aloud metacognitively or non-metacognitively should be based on the research question(s) being asked and the level of detail required to answer them sufficiently. In general, non-metacognitive think-alouds should provide enough detail to answer most research questions. Only when it is necessary to probe participants' justifications should metacognitive think-alouds be needed. Imagine an experimental study on interlanguage pragmatics that probed learners' pragmatic knowledge through a written discourse completion task (WDCT). If the research question were, "To what extent do advanced L2 learners of Spanish make native-like pragmatic judgments regarding form of address?" then quantitative data from the DCT could be used to answer the question. Qualitative data in the form of non-metacognitive think-alouds could be used to explore similarities and differences between native speakers and L2 learners' thought processes. However, if the research question were, "What factors do L2 learners and native speakers of Spanish take into account when choosing between informal and formal forms of address?" it would probably be necessary to collect more detailed, metacognitive think-alouds that would reveal the learners' and native speakers' justifications regarding form of address. In this case, it is important to note that the verbalization instructions should also specify the level of detail that participants are expected to provide. A sample instruction might specify: "Please say out loud all of the factors you are considering as you decide whether the informal or the formal form of address would be more appropriate in each situation described."

All of the SLA studies on reactivity to date except one (Sachs & Polio, 2007) allowed participants to think aloud in their L1, their L2, or a combination of the two, as they preferred. Therefore, there is not sufficient data to determine whether language of verbalization has an effect on reactivity, and further research in this area is needed. To ensure that participants are able to provide as complete a report of their thoughts as possible, it is advisable to allow both the L1 and the L2 to be used in think-alouds. This may be especially important for lower-proficiency L2 learners, who may have difficulty expressing their thoughts if they are not allowed to do so in their L1. The language of report should be restricted to the L2 only (1) in cases where the research question necessitates it or (2) in cases where the only language shared by the participants and the researchers is the L2. In the latter case, the requirement that participants think aloud in their L2 is purely for practical reasons – to facilitate data analysis – and should be avoided if at all possible.

Timing and Think-Alouds

Based on the literature in cognitive psychology (Ericsson & Simon, 1983, 1994) as well as the meta-analysis presented in the previous chapter, it is clear that thinking aloud generally increases the time it takes participants to complete a given task. Therefore, in studies where reaction time is a dependent variable under investigation, the use of think-alouds is not advisable, since it will likely inflate reaction time measurements.

Recording Think-Alouds

For most SLA research, audio recordings of participants' think-alouds can be obtained with either handheld digital voice recorders or computerized recording software, which make it easy to conduct research in both classrooms and laboratories. The recordings obtained are generally clear enough to enable both word-level and segmental analysis. Researchers investigating aspects of interlanguage phonology will likely want to record participants in a soundproof booth with higher-quality recording equipment that will enable acoustic analysis with software such as Praat.

Researchers working under the paradigm of conversation analysis generally supplement their audio recordings with video recordings to capture gestures and other non-verbal cues unavailable in a simple audio recording. The type of recording(s) should be selected taking into account the research questions being investigated and the theoretical assumptions of the study.

Ensuring Validity

This chapter concludes with a series of recommendations that researchers should follow when collecting think-alouds to ensure their validity. As discussed at the beginning of the chapter, it is crucial that all participants receive uniform verbalization instructions and that they be allowed to complete a "warm-up task" during which they practice thinking aloud. Although the warm-up task may be either non-verbal (e.g. arithmetic) or verbal, it is important that the warm-up task not prime the participants for the target structure that will be tested in the study. After the warm-up session, participants should have the opportunity to ask questions and clarify any doubts they may have about the procedure.

During the study, the researcher should periodically remind participants to continue thinking aloud. In computer-based studies, such as Bowles (2008) and Sanz et al. (2009), these reminders can appear on the computer screen at key points in the task. The researcher should also circulate during the experiment to provide manipulation checks, reminding participants to think aloud whenever they pause more than momentarily. Providing manipulation checks ensures that all participants think aloud consistently during all parts of the task.

As a final safeguard to ensure that the data collected from participants who think aloud is valid, it is advisable to include a small control group of participants who complete the same language tasks silently (without the requirement to think aloud). The need for a control group is reinforced by the findings of the meta-analysis presented in Chapter 3, which unveiled several factors that appear to affect whether thinking aloud causes reactivity. The caution issued by Leow and Morgan-Short (2004, p. 50) in the first SLA study on reactivity is perhaps more relevant than ever before:

> [G]iven the many variables that potentially impact the issue of reactivity in SLA research methodology, it is suggested that studies employing concurrent data-elicitation procedures include a control group that does not perform verbal reports as one way of addressing this issue.

The rationale behind having a control group is that if scores on post-task assessments are statistically similar in the silent and think-aloud groups, it can be concluded that verbalization did not have reactive effects and, by extension, that thinking aloud did not substantially alter participants' cognitive processes.

A summary of the steps in using think-alouds in language research is provided in Figure 4.1.

Before the study
- Decide if think-alouds are appropriate to use with the type of language task you plan to use.
- Decide on the type and language of verbalization you want to elicit.
- Include an indication that voice samples will be recorded in the informed consent document.

During the study
- In the think-aloud instructions provided to participants:
  - Include a rationale for having participants think aloud.
  - Provide general instructions to participants about how to think aloud.
- Provide learners with a warm-up task to let them practice thinking aloud before they move on to the experimental task.
- Record think-alouds using appropriate equipment to ensure the necessary level of detail.
- To ensure validity:
  - Verify that participants in think-aloud groups continue thinking aloud throughout the task. Remind them of this as necessary.
  - Include a small control group that performs the same tasks without thinking aloud as a check on validity.

Figure 4.1 Using Think-Alouds in Data Collection

5 Data Analysis Considerations

This chapter discusses factors that should be taken into account when analyzing think-aloud data. Several examples are provided, although by no means are the contents of this chapter exhaustive with regard to the ways in which think-aloud data could be analyzed.

A study's research questions and guiding theoretical background are the most central considerations in data analysis. All aspects of data analysis, from transcription to coding, and concluding with the qualitative and/or quantitative methods, are driven by the theoretical framework and ultimate goals of the study.

Transcription

The first decision that must be made in the data analysis process is how to transcribe the think-alouds. There are many different transcription conventions in SLA and the choice of which to use is motivated mainly by the theoretical framework of the study. For instance, studies based on conversation-analytic approaches use a detailed transcription system that includes periods of silence indicated in tenths of a second, micropauses, indications of rising and falling intonation contours, and information about non-verbal aspects of communication, such as gestures, which are typically recorded by video (Markee, 2005).

The excerpt below, which covers just seven seconds of data, is taken from Markee (2005, p. 365) to show the level of detail that can be expected in a conversation-analytic transcription.

055 L10:	ok uh:m (.3) also is a f<u>oo</u>d for- is a f<u>oo</u>d for
056 L9:	_____
057 L10:	f<u>i</u>sh/e/, and uh ((L10 _makes a chopping motion_
058	_with her right hand, emphasizing_
059	_the words "f<u>oo</u>d" and "f<u>oo</u>d for"_

060   *fish/e/". L10 ends her turn*
061   *with her right hand held up*
062   *vertically, palm open))*

In this case, the colon in line 055 "uh:m" indicates the lengthening of the vowel, and the subsequent numbers in parenthesis indicate that the speaker then paused for .3 seconds before continuing. Underlined letters indicate marked stress on that portion of the word or phrase, and the description in parenthesis and italics that extends from line 058 to line 062 indicates the non-verbal behaviors the speaker uses to help make her meaning clear. Transcribing in such fine-grained detail can be extremely time-consuming. Markee (2005, p. 364) cites a one minute, three second portion of interaction which, when transcribed using this system, took up 130 lines of text and required 15 hours to produce. Clearly, the time investment is worthwhile only if the research questions require such detail.

Studies framed in sociocultural theory and cognitivist approaches to SLA do not tend to use such a detailed transcription system. These transcripts tend to include no more than word-level detail unless the research questions specifically require information about phonetic representations, intonation, or other phenomena not captured in word-level transcriptions. The excerpt below, reproduced from the appendix of Leow and Bowles (2005), is a transcript of a think-aloud from Leow (2001b). The participant is reading a passage in the L2 (Spanish) that includes many instances of the targeted form, the formal imperative:

Um, OK. Uh, preventative medicine. How to live a healthy life. First, you have to eat well. Um, *cada día toma fruta y verduras.* [each day eat fruit and vegetables.] Each day eat fruit and vegetables, meat, and uh, *pescado* [fish], I think that's, um, poultry. Uh, two or three eggs per week, milk or cheese, uh, for dairy food. Um, let's see. *Haga y ponga*, [Do and put] hmm. Well, *ponga* [put, formal imperative] kind of looks like *pongo* [put, 1st person singular present] which is, um, *pon*, or *poner, ponerse* [to put on, reflexive] which is able. So, um, and *haga* [do, formal imperative] kind of looks like uh, kinda looks like uh, *hacer* [to do] or something. So you can list, uh, *puerta* [door]. I thought that was door, but so you can list in door of *nevera* [refrigerator]. Ok, I don't really know what that sentence means, so I'll put a little star by it or something. Um. I don't really recognize these verb forms either so I better circle any unknown verb forms so I'll circle *haga* [do, formal imperative] and *ponga* [put, formal

imperative], except I think *ponga* is, um, I think *ponga* might be
a *tú* [informal you] command. Anyway.

As the excerpt of this transcript shows, there is much less detail than
in the fine-grained conversation-analytic transcript from Markee
(2005). Italics are used to mark words said in the participant's L2
(Spanish) but apart from that convention, no special attention is
given to intonation, timing, or pauses, and no information about
non-verbal cues is provided.

But whatever the level of detail, transcription is time-consuming.
The researcher, research assistants, and any others who are involved
in the transcription process should all be trained in the transcription
system to be used. Where multiple people are involved in transcribing the data, it is important that inter-rater reliability be calculated or
that a socialization procedure be followed to ensure that all transcribers are applying the same conventions and are doing so consistently. Clearly, it is essential that transcribers understand the
language(s) used in the think-alouds. As the meta-analysis presented
in Chapter 3 shows, to date studies have almost exclusively allowed
learners to verbalize in either their L1 (most often English), in their
L2, or in a combination of the two. In such cases, where the participants speak only two languages, it is relatively easy to identify transcribers with the requisite language knowledge. In cases where
participants are from a variety of L1 backgrounds (as is often the
case in ESL research) it may be necessary to find a team of research
assistants to transcribe and translate the think-alouds, since each
individual is likely to be familiar with only a subset of the languages
represented by the participants.

Ensuring Representativeness

Once the think-alouds have been transcribed, it is important that
they be reviewed to ensure representativeness. This is especially true
regarding type of report. Even given careful instructions and manipulation checks during data collection, all participants may not have
verbalized according to the initial instructions they received. For
instance, type of report was one independent variable in Bowles
(2008). It was therefore essential that all of the participants' think-
alouds be coded accurately as either metacognitive or non-metacognitive. The researcher listened to all the participants' verbal reports
and coded them in a binary fashion, in keeping with Bowles and
Leow (2005). If a participant provided justifications for 50 per cent
or more of the paths chosen, his or her report was coded as

metacognitive. Conversely, if a participant provided justifications for fewer than 50 per cent of the paths chosen, his or her report was coded as non-metacognitive. In practice, however, participants were never near this 50 per cent cutoff. The verbal reports coded as non-metacognitive contained justifications for 0–20 per cent of the paths chosen, whereas those coded as metacognitive contained justifications for 70–100 per cent of the paths. Of the 125 total verbal reports in Bowles (2008), eight (approximately 6 per cent of the dataset) were reclassified. Nevertheless, the importance of this quality control measure should not be understated. If representativeness is not verified, there is a serious threat to the study's internal validity.

Coding

Just as think-alouds can be collected to answer research questions in a variety of strands of SLA research, as reviewed in Chapter 1, they can be coded in a number of ways. Many researchers employ a mixed-methods approach, whereby some aspect(s) of the think-alouds is/are quantified and excerpts of the think-alouds themselves are used to exemplify or provide further insight to answer the research questions. The ways in which data from think-alouds are quantified depend on the research questions and the research tradition, and there is no one correct or appropriate way to code the data. Coding schemes must be developed and tailored to fit the research questions being investigated.

The examples provided below are taken from a range of studies and are intended to demonstrate a variety of coding schemes that have been developed for use with think-alouds.

Coding Example 1: Rosa and O'Neill (1999)

Rosa and O'Neill (1999) investigated the relationship between awareness and L2 intake. In the study, L2 learners of Spanish were exposed to contrary-to-fact conditionals in the past, and type of exposure was manipulated by means of two variables: ± formal instruction on the conditional and ± directions to search for rules. All participants were instructed to think aloud while completing the task:

> In this experiment we are interested in what you think about when you complete this task. In order to find out, we are going to ask you to THINK ALOUD as you put together the puzzles, from the time you start the task until you finish the task. We

would like you to talk CONSTANTLY. We don't want you to try to plan out what you say or try to explain to us what you're saying. Just act as if you are alone in the room speaking to yourself. What's most important is that you keep talking, and talk clearly and loudly enough into your microphone. We will not be able to help you in any way. *You can think aloud either in Spanish or in English.*

(Rosa & O'Neill 1999, p. 525).

The think-alouds were then used to assess the participants' level of awareness of the targeted linguistic form. Rosa and O'Neill chose to use think-alouds to gather these data based on the body of literature in cognitive psychology that links awareness with the ability to verbalize a subjective experience (e.g. Allport, 1988; Carr & Curran, 1994; Nissen & Bullemer, 1987).

The researchers coded each think-aloud into one of three categories, based on the highest level of awareness demonstrated: (1) awareness at the level of noticing (+N), (2) awareness at the level of understanding (+U), or (3) no explicit report of awareness/no verbal report (NVR).

For Rosa and O'Neill (1999, p. 529): "[A]wareness at the level of noticing, or [+N] (Schmidt, 1990, 1993, 1994, 1995), was operationalized as a verbal reference to the target structure without any mention of rules." A higher-level of awareness, awareness at the level of understanding, or [+U] (Schmidt, 1990, 1993, 1994, 1995), was operationalized as

> an explicit formulation of the rule underlying the target structure. In order for a report to be categorized as [+U], the participant had to explicitly make a connection between present or past time frames and the corresponding verb forms (imperfect subjunctive or past perfect subjunctive, respectively).
>
> (Rosa & O'Neill, 1999, p. 530)

The third category, no explicit report of awareness/no verbal report (NVR) was used to mark the think-alouds of participants who simply "read . . . aloud the sentences in the experimental task without giving any verbal signal that either the verb in the target structure or the rule governing it had been cognitively registered" (Rosa & O'Neill, 1999, p. 530).

Results of ANOVAs indicated that learners whose think-alouds demonstrated the highest level of awareness (+U) scored significantly higher on post-tests of the targeted form than did learners who merely noticed the form (+N) or who were in the NVR group. In addition, there was no significant difference in post-test scores between learners who merely noticed the form (+N) and those who were in the NVR group.

The researchers then referred back to the cognitive psychology literature on awareness to decide how to interpret their findings. Although cognitive psychologists have linked awareness and self-report, Allport (1988) has indicated that lack of report cannot be taken to be synonymous with lack of awareness. If participants do not report awareness, then, it could be that they are unaware, or, alternatively, that they were aware but did not verbalize that awareness. Given this caution, Rosa and O'Neill (1999) do not refer to the NVR participants as "unaware" but rather make claims only about the two reporting groups (+N and +U).

Coding Example 2: Seng and Hashim (2006)

The second coding example comes from the large body of empirical studies that has used think-alouds to investigate strategy use. Seng and Hashim (2006) investigated the extent and functions of L1 use in L2 reading comprehension. Specifically, the researchers questioned (1) with what frequency the L1 was used during L2 reading and (2) which reading strategies were most used in the L1. Four students studying at a Malaysian university (L1 Malay) read an English text and were instructed to verbalize their thoughts and to "use whatever language they felt most comfortable using" (p. 34). Prior to coding the think-alouds, the researchers identified a tentative list of reading strategies based on previous strategy research (N. J. Anderson, 1991; Block, 1986; Jimenez et al., 1996; Steinberg et al., 1991). Then the think-alouds were coded iteratively, with the researchers making reference to the list of strategies. At this stage, strategies that appeared in the list but not in the transcripts were deleted and those that appeared in the transcripts but not in the list were added. Only once the finalized list had been established was the final coding completed. Two independent raters were trained on the coding procedures, receiving both the finalized list of strategies as well as a definition and an example of each strategy. The raters were then asked to code the strategies found in the transcripts.

Quantitative analyses, using descriptive statistics, were provided to answer the research questions. To answer the first research question, how frequently the L1 was used, each instance of strategy use was coded according to whether it occurred in the L1 or L2, and a percentage of L1 use was calculated for each participant, as well as for all participants overall. L1 use ranged from 25.9 per cent to 35.5 per cent, with a mean of 32.2 per cent of strategies across all participants being carried out in the L1.

To answer the second research question, all of the instances of L1 use were arranged in order of frequency by strategy. Translation was the most common strategy involving L1, and it consisted of 31.66 per cent of the total number of strategy uses where the L1 was involved. In descending order of frequency, the other strategies that occurred in the L1 in more than 5 per cent of cases were paraphrasing (13.07 per cent), questioning (12.56 per cent), guessing (9.55 per cent), inferencing (8.54 per cent), and word recognition (5.03 per cent). Conversely, some strategies, such as using prior knowledge and evaluating comprehension, rarely involved L1 use.

An excerpt of the coder training materials, as presented in the Appendix of Seng and Hashim (2006), is provided below. Four strategies, of the 18 that appeared in the finalized list, are shown here:

Strategy name and code:	Rereading (RS 1 Rerdg)
Description:	Read again a portion of the text that has already been read.
	(a) – entire paragraph verbatim (b) – entire sentence verbatim (c) – parts of sentence verbatim
Examples:	<u>Some children grab the treat the moment he's out the door</u> *out the door.* Erh, *some children grab the treat the moment he's out the door.*
Strategy name and code:	Summarizing (RS 2 Sumrs)
Description:	Summarize what is thought as the information found in a segment (a paragraph or at least three sentences long) of the text after a discussion on that segment.
Examples:	(After a paragraph is read) I think the paragraph, erh, erh, scientist who erh, do a research and they want to know the future of the children
Strategy name and code:	Translation (RS 10 Trans)
Description:	Translate a word or a portion of text to the L1

(w)= word
(i) = idea

Examples: She launched her campaign claiming
                                   Dia melancarkan kempen dia,
                                   launched campaign

Strategy name and code: Guessing (RS 11 Guess)
Description: Guess the probable meaning/pronun-
                                   ciation of a word or guess the proba-
                                   ble meaning of a portion of text.

                                   (w) = word
                                   (i) = idea

Examples: *Moaning what ahh, moaning?*
                                   (Question)
                                   Maybe social chat (Guess)

Coding Example 3: Woodfield (2008)

In recent years, verbal reports, both retrospective and concurrent, have been used to probe the interlanguage pragmatic competence of L2 learners. Woodfield (2008) tests the validity and authenticity of a WDCT by having native English-speaking participants complete the task in pairs while thinking aloud. A central research question was to determine the cognitive processes English native speakers used while responding to the 18 scenarios presented in the WDCT.

The transcripts of the think-alouds were analyzed using Content Analysis (Krippendorf, 2003; Weber, 1990) to reduce the discussion in the verbal reports to a finite set of coding categories. Five categories were identified in the data and described for the purposes of rater training as follows:

Orientating: Orientating to: the social context of the discourse
                 situation; the situated nature of [the] discourse
                 situation within a speech event; to [the] decision
                 as to whether a request would be made
Planning: Planning of responses in relation to sociocontex-
                 tual situation
Solving: Proposal of hypotheses as possible responses to
                 written task
Reviewing/   Metacognitive reflections on task and task
refelecting: responses including: reasons for hypotheses;
                 reflections on identities and roles within and

outside of research task; familiarity/unfamiliarity
with the discourse situation

Evaluating: Evaluation of: appropriateness of response; of
own/partner's hypotheses; of task difficulty.

(Woodfield 2008, p. 69)

The analysis was descriptive in nature and revealed four types of
deficiencies of the WDCT as perceived by the native English-speaking participants. Each of the four types of deficiencies was described
and exemplified qualitatively using excerpts from the think-alouds.

The first type of deficiency in the WDCT is labeled "Attend to
interactive nature of the speech event." In such cases, as participants
responded to the WDCT, they appeared to resist the instructions to
respond to the situation in just one turn and instead tended to construct responses in a more lengthy way, taking into account any of a
number of interactive factors. The WDCT task, participants' written
response, and excerpt from their think-aloud are reproduced below.
In the think-aloud data, "A" and "B" are used to mark the two interlocutors.

Excerpt 1. Task A1: Lift
Discourse situation
Your car has broken down and you would like someone to drive
you home from the supermarket. There are no buses that go to
your home. You see some other people who live in your street
(who you do not know) standing near the exit. Ask them to drive
you home.

Written response (EN3)
"Excuse me, don't you live in X street? I don't suppose you're
going home are you or could drop me off please as my car has
broken down."

Concurrent verbal report (EN3)

1 B: "Oh yes, you're at number 7" or whatever, depends on
        whether you'd
2   pursue it any more, wouldn't it?
3 A: I suppose it'd depend how many people were there that I
        know as
4   well. If there's only one person there that I recognize then
        I'd probably
5   pursue them more. You know if they didn't immediately
        acknowledge then

6   I'd just carry on explaining who I was and where I was from.

7   Mm. Because as you say it may be a group of people and they're just with

8   some friends. And that would then be followed by you know "Where are

9   you off to, by the way? I just wondered, are you on your way home?"

10   Intervening data

11   I would go over and say "don't you live in . . ." whatever road it is that

12   you live at . . .

13   Yeah

14   A: And see what their reaction is to that

15   So you'd be reading a lot of non verbal probably in there, their reaction to

16   that. I think that'd be important to establish that before you get any

17   further about "my car's broken down" or anything like that.

18   Intervening data

19   B: So "Excuse me, don't you live in X street?" Because we haven't actually

20   said here that that's where we live. Have we?

21   A: No. But I suppose that depends on their reaction again, doesn't it?

22   B: Their reaction yeah.

23   A: Because they might recognize you.

24   Say "Don't you live in X street?" and then depending on a yes or a no . . .

25   A: Yeah

26   B: "Oh I thought I'd seen you around yes I live at number 4." So this is

27   really a follow on, I mean this is a separate part of the discourse here

28   definitely isn't it? I mean you'd need to close the speech marks there I

29   think because this is dependent on the response to the first half. "I don't

30   suppose you're going home are you, or could drop me off please, because

31   my car's broken down."

32   That's all right.

33   Okay, yeah

34 I'd say that.
35 Brilliant

(Woodfield, 2008, pp. 52–53)

The author uses this excerpt to show that the participants are considering a number of hypothetical situations in constructing their response and in fact go to some effort to limit their response to just a one-turn sequence.

The second type of deficiency was labeled "Attend to lack of contextual detail in the discourse situation." This category encompassed think-alouds where participants indicated implicitly or explicitly that they needed more contextual detail to respond to the task. The discourse task, written response, and excerpt of the participants' think-aloud are reproduced below:

Excerpt 3. Task C1: Extension
Discourse situation
You have been asked by your lecturer to give a seminar paper but you need more time. You go to see her to ask her for extra time to prepare your paper. Ask for an extension.

Written response (EN1)
I've got a problem. I'm not going to be able to give the seminar paper on Tuesday. Could we make it the following week?

Concurrent verbal report (EN1)

1 There's not enough information there.
2 You'd have to give a reason.
3 I think first of all you know when you ask the lecturer is it before the
4 deadline, on the day? Presumably you've already discussed what the
5 paper's going to be about, what the seminar's going to be about. But I
6 think this would really depend on when you were asking for an extension. If
7 you were well in advance of it, a couple of weeks in advance, I think I could do
8 it. If it was the day before I just feel, you know . . . again I don't think that
9 situation would arise. And and also you know you'd have to say why.
10 Again like if it was a couple of weeks before, presumably the reason . . .

11   well saying you need more time, not that you have another

12   engagement or you've got something else you have to do.

13   Intervening data

14   And how much more time anyway? How much more time are you

15   going to ask for? Because that would affect it also

16   Mm.

17 A: I think there's too many variables for the situation to be clear.

(Woodfield, 2008, pp. 55–56)

The third type of deficiency was labeled "Attend to inauthenticity of DCT" and this category was used in cases where the participants specifically commented on some aspect of the task not reflecting real life.

Excerpt 6. Task C2: Book
Discourse situation
You realize you need an important book for your essay. The book is not available in the library. You know your lecturer has a copy of the book you need. Ask to borrow the book.

Written response (EN2)
A: Sorry to bother you I'm in the middle of the assignment on teacher education, and I've just found out that x isn't in the library. I think you said you had a copy. Would it be all right if I borrowed it for a couple of days?

Concurrent verbal report (EN2)

1 A: Mm (reading). "You've missed the last bus home and you know your

2   lecturer's going your way" . . . so actually . . . I mean in a way with these

3   situations the only way to avoid the artificiality of the other person not

4   reacting in the middle of the long speech is probably in order to fulfil a

5   task you actually need to say, do things not in the order you might

6   naturally do them and to say "Sorry to bother you but could I borrow

7   your copy of X?" and then explain why. And in fact once you have said

8   "could I borrow your copy of the book?" then that's the
     task completed.

(Woodfield, 2008, pp. 58–59)

The final type of deficiency identified was labeled as "Reconstruct the DCT to create an authentic discourse context" and the excerpts of think-alouds in this category show instances in which participants reconstructed the WDCT to create what they perceived to be a more authentic discourse context.

> Excerpt 7. Task D2: Hospital
> Discourse situation
> You are at home, looking after a friend's child. An elderly neighbour has had a bad fall. She comes to your door and says she is badly hurt and wants you to take her to the local hospital. She asks for your help. (She says . . .)
>
> Written response (EN1)
> Oh (name) I've hurt myself and I think I need to go to the hospital.
>
> Concurrent verbal report (EN1)

1   A: I think the problem with this again is that it wouldn't be
        . . . it would
2   be a dialogue it wouldn't be a straightforward . . .
3   B: Wouldn't be a straight forward request, yeah. You'd
        have your
4   flustered neighbour saying "Oh X . . ." and you would
        see and hear
5   distress and you would respond to that . . .
6   A: "Are you all right?"
7   B: "Are you all right," yeah. "No I don't think I am, I fell
        over the cat." And
8   you know "I've hurt my leg,"
9   A: Again I think you would be the one to suggest that they
        go to the
10   hospital
11 B: Yeah
12 A: xxx this isn't easy
13 B: No, I thought this might be difficult.

(Woodfield, 2008, pp. 59–60)

As the coding procedures for think-alouds in these three studies have shown, there are many ways to make use of verbal report data. As the use of think-alouds continues to expand to new areas of SLA research and to address different research questions, researchers will need to be increasingly innovative in designing coding schemes that are tailored to meet their needs.

Inter-Coder Reliability

No matter what coding scheme is adopted, it is essential that researchers calculate and report inter-coder reliability on at least a subset of the think-aloud data. For efficiency, often a small percentage of the transcripts (10–25 per cent) is selected at random and independently coded by another researcher, based on the coding scheme provided.

There are several ways that inter-coder reliability can be calculated. The least complex and most widely used means is a simple percentage of agreement. In this procedure, the number of identical ratings obtained by two raters is divided by the total number of ratings to obtain a percentage of agreement. One criticism of this method is that it does not take into account the fact that some agreements may have been the result of chance. A more sophisticated measure that accounts for agreement occurring by chance is known as Cohen's kappa (κ). Unlike the simple percentage method, Cohen's kappa is reported on a scale of 0–1 and is interpreted like a correlation coefficient, with values closer to zero indicating less agreement and values closer to one indicating more agreement. Researchers should strive to have kappa values of .8 or higher on each of the coding variables.

6   Conclusion

In this final chapter, I return to the controversy surrounding think-alouds with which the book began. Swain (2006b) sums up the controversy over verbal reports, writing: "What do verbal protocols represent? . . . [Are they] brain dumps . . . or are they part of what constitutes development and learning?" (p. 97). Until now, the response to Swain's question has largely been answered anecdotally, albeit differently, based on the theoretical perspective of the researcher providing the response.

Researchers coming from a cognitivist or information processing perspective tend to view think-alouds as "a trace of the cognitive processes that people attend to while doing a task" (Swain, 2006b, p. 99). Think-alouds therefore are seen as a window into cognitive processes and are used as a data collection tool. Researchers coming from the perspective of sociocultural theory hold a fundamentally different view of think-alouds, based on the work of Vygotsky (1987), according to whom "thought is not merely expressed in words; it comes into existence through them" (p. 240). For these researchers, verbalization leads to learning and the very act of verbalizing changes the thought process.

Based on the findings of the meta-analysis of studies presented in this book, it is possible to provide at least a few empirically-based answers to the debate over think-alouds. Most importantly, it is clear that the answer to the question is not one-size-fits-all. That is, think-alouds may have different functions under different circumstances. Reactivity is not unidimensional; rather, it depends on a host of factors and can either be positive (improving task performance) or negative (hindering task performance).

Based on the evidence available to date, it appears that in some cases verbal reports can indeed be a source of learning, as sociocultural theory would suggest. For instance, participants who thought aloud non-metacognitively scored moderately higher ($d = .67$) on receptive tests of form learning than did participants who completed the same task silently (Table 3.4). This result suggests that verbalizing facilitated form learning, at least as measured by receptive tests. On tests of productive form learning, however, thinking aloud had a small, detrimental effect ($d = -.12$).

By the same token, the small effect sizes of $d \leq .5$ in 81 per cent of the effect size calculations indicate that any post-test differences between silent and think-aloud groups are generally quite small. Additionally, in 86 per cent of the effect size calculations, the 95 per cent confidence interval overlaps zero, indicating that the d value is not significantly different from zero. This finding suggests that verbal reports can reliably be used as a data collection tool.

Future Research Directions

More research is clearly needed overall in examining reactivity in conjunction with verbal tasks, given the paucity of reactivity research with language tasks as compared to non-verbal and problem-solving tasks. Empirical studies are needed to test the sources of between-study variance identified in the meta-analysis to determine to what extent they affect reactivity. Some of the variance could be attributed to expected sources, such as type of report (metacognitive vs. non-metacognitive), which has been discussed at length in the psychology literature (Ericsson & Simon, 1993). The other sources of between-study variance that were identified, L2 proficiency and explicitness of instruction, are unique to the language research context. Future research is clearly needed to determine how verbalizing affects learners (1) at different proficiency levels and (2) in conjunction with more and less explicit instruction.

The systematic coding and analysis of reactivity studies that was conducted as part of the meta-analysis revealed several areas that, despite their theoretical importance, have been under-investigated. Specifically, lacking are studies that examine the effect of using just one language (either L1 or L2) in thinking aloud. This is because most of the studies conducted so far have examined the reactive effects of think-alouds when participants were allowed to select either the L1 or the L2, or to use a combination of the two languages, in their reports. Certainly, this is a gap in the research that should be filled.

Similarly, some task types have been investigated more heavily than others with regard to reactivity. Topping the list are studies that have examined the reactivity of think-alouds on reading ($n = 6$) and grammar learning tasks ($n = 7$). But the effect of think-alouds on the writing process has only been investigated in two unique sample studies, making it untenable to draw firm conclusions about reactivity with this task type.

The findings of the meta-analysis have important implications for researchers from a variety of different theoretical perspectives. Crucially, a variety of factors seem to play a role in determining whether or not verbalization is reactive on a given task. What is true for one task type may not be for another.

Since the first reactivity study in SLA (Leow & Morgan-Short, 2004) was conducted less than a decade ago, there are undoubtedly more questions than answers about verbal reports and reactivity. The results of the meta-analysis stress the importance of including a (silent) control group in the design of any study using verbal reports as a data collection tool. This safeguard allows the researcher to determine whether verbalizing caused significantly different task performance compared to silent participants. The findings also highlight the need for more fine-grained research to determine under what circumstances verbalizations are likely to accurately reflect processing and in what circumstances they are likely to serve as a learning tool or as a hindrance to learning.

Appendix A
Studies Included in the Meta-Analysis

Bowles, M. (2008). Task type and reactivity of verbal reports in SLA: A first look at a task other than reading. *Studies in Second Language Acquisition, 30*(3), 359–387.

Bowles, M., & Leow, R. P. (2005). Reactivity and type of verbal report in SLA research methodology: Expanding the scope of investigation. *Studies in Second Language Acquisition, 27*(3), 415–440.

Lass, U., Klettke, W., Lüer, G., & Ruhlender, P. (1991). Does thinking aloud influence the structure of cognitive processes? In R. Schmid & D. Zambarbieri (Eds.), *Oculomotor control and cognitive processes* (pp. 385–396). Amsterdam: North-Holland Publishing Co.

Leow, R. P., & Morgan-Short, K. (2004). To think aloud or not to think aloud: The issue of reactivity in SLA research methodology. *Studies in Second Language Acquisition, 26*(1), 35–57.

Mathews, R. C., Buss, R. R., Stanley, W. B., Blanchard-Fields, F., Cho, J. R., & Druhan, B. (1989). Role of implicit and explicit processes in learning from examples: A synergistic effect. *Journal of Experimental Psychology: Learning, Memory, and Cognition, 15*, 1083–1100.

Polio, C., & Wang, J. (in review). Another look at the reactivity of concurrent verbal protocols in second language reading research: A replication of Leow and Morgan-Short (2004). *Studies in Second Language Acquisition.*

Rossomondo, A. E. (2007). The role of lexical temporal indicators and text interaction format in the incidental acquisition of the Spanish future tense. *Studies in Second Language Acquisition, 29*(1), 39–66.

[a]Sachs, R., & Polio, C. (2007). Learners' uses of two types of written feedback on an L2 writing revision task. *Studies in Second Language Acquisition, 29*(1), 67–100.

Sachs, R., & Suh, B. R. (2007). Textually enhanced recasts, learner awareness, and L2 outcomes in synchronous computer-mediated interaction. In A. Mackey (Ed.), *Conversational interaction in second language acquisition: A collection of empirical studies* (pp. 197–227). Oxford: Oxford University Press.

[a]Sanz, C., Lin, H.-J., Lado, B., Bowden, H. W., & Stafford, C. A. (2009). Concurrent verbalizations, pedagogical conditions, and reactivity: Two CALL studies. *Language Learning, 59*(1), 33–71.

Short, E. J., Schatschneider, C., Cuddy, C. L., Evans, S. W., Dellick, D. M., & Basili, L. A. (1991). The effect of thinking aloud on the problem solving performance of bright, average, learning disabled, and developmentally handicapped students. *Contemporary Educational Psychology, 16*, 139–153.

Yoshida, M. (2008). Think-aloud protocols and type of reading task: The issue of reactivity in L2 reading research. In M. Bowles, R. Foote, S. Perpiñán, & R. Bhatt (Eds.), *Selected proceedings of the 2007 Second Language Research Forum* (pp. 199–209). Somerville, MA: Cascadilla Proceedings Project.

Note

a Each of these published research reports presents data and findings from two unique sample studies.

Appendix B

Summary of Unique Sample Studies[a]

Study Report/ Treatment Groups	N	Language of Report	Report Type	Language of Task	Type of Task	Explicitness	Measure of Form Learning	Measure of Text Comprehension	Measure of Latency
SLA Studies **Bowles (2008)**									
Non-Metacognitive + Explicit Feedback	33	L1/L2	NM	L2	GL	+E	P[b] -.49, -.33	–	ToT[c] .02
Metacognitive + Explicit Feedback	33	L1/L2	M	L2	GL	+E	P -.68, -.53	–	ToT .86
Non-Metacognitive + Implicit Feedback	36	L1/L2	NM	L2	GL	-E	P -.15, -.35	–	ToT –
Metacognitive + Implicit Feedback	36	L1/L2	M	L2	GL	-E	P -.01, .14	–	ToT –
Leow and Morgan-Short (2004)	38	L1/L2	NM	L2	R	–	R P .37 .06	R .34	–
Bowles and Leow (2005) Non-Metacognitive	18	L1/L2	NM	L2	R	–	P .25, .18[d]	R .55	ToT .96

Study	n			L2						
Metacognitive	10	L1/L2	M	L2	R	—	P .10, −.20		R −.46	ToT 1.60
Sachs and Sub (2007)	13	L1/L2	NM	L2	I	—	R .99	P .08	—	ToT[e] .03
Sachs and Polio (2007), Experiment 1	15	L2	NM	L2	W	—	P −.24		—	—
Sachs and Polio (2007), Experiment 2	16	L2	NM	L2	W	—	P .06		—	—
Yoshida (2008)										
Embedded	10	L1/L2	M	L2	R	—	—		P .33	ToT 1.23
Outline	9	L1/L2	M	L2	R	—	—		P −.32	ToT .96
Sanz et al. (2009), Experiment 1	13	L1/L2	M	L2	GL	+E	R[f] .21, .05	P −.27	—	RT[g] .56, .83, .51
Sanz et al. (2009), Experiment 2	11	L1/L2	M	L2	GL	−E	R .84, .86	P .85	—	RT −.04, .40, −.15
Rossomondo (2007)										
Passage with LTIs	12	n.r.	NM	L2	R	—	R 1.35	P .56	R −.27	—
Passage without LTIs	9	n.r.	NM	L2	R	—	R .83	P 1.80	R .18	—

Study Report/ Treatment Groups	N	Language of Report	Report Type	Language of Task	Type of Task	Explicitness	Measure of Form Learning	Measure of Text Comprehension	Measure of Latency
Polio and Wang (in review)	15	L1/L2	NM	L2	R	–	R –.54 / P –.28	R –.98	–
Non-SLA Studies									
Lass et al. (1991)	35	L1	NM	L1	ML	–	P –.29	–	ToT –.56
Mathews et al. (1989), Experiment 2	168	L1	M	L1	GL	–	P .26	–	–
Short et al. (1991)	94	L1	M	L1	ML	–	P[h] .83, 1.08, .80, .47	–	–

Notes

Positive d values in the *measure of form learning* and *measure of text comprehension* columns indicate that the think-aloud group performed better on the given test than the silent group did. Positive d values in the *measure of latency* column indicate that the think-aloud group took longer to complete the task than the silent group did. Negative values indicate the opposite.

a NM = non-metacognitive, M = metacognitive, R = reading, W = writing, GL = grammar learning, I = interaction, ML = meta-language, +E = Explicit, –E = Implicit, R = receptive, P = productive, ToT = time on task, RT = reaction time, LTI = lexical temporal indicator, n.r. = not reported.

b For Bowles (2008), the first effect size is for the comparison between the silent control and the verbalization group for item learning; the second is for system learning.

c For latency measurements, the groups were analyzed only according to type of report (metacognitive *vs.* non-metacognitive) so there are only two effect sizes.

d For Bowles and Leow (2005), the first effect size is for the comparison between the silent control and the verbalization group for item learning; the second is for system learning.

e The values from Sachs and Suh (2007) are for time spent in treatment.

f The first receptive test was aural interpretation and the second was a grammaticality judgment test.

g Reaction times were separately computed and compared to those of a silent control group on three measures, in order – aural interpretation, grammaticality judgment, and production.

h Effect sizes were calculated for the verbal analogies only. The four effect sizes given, in order, refer to bright, average, learning disabled, and developmentally handicapped children's scores under the think-aloud condition compared to their own performance completing the analogies silently.

Notes

3 Features that Make a Task Amenable to Think-Aloud

1. Rhenius and Deffner (1990), Russo et al. (1989), and Stratman and Hamp-Lyons (1994) could not be included in the meta-analysis because the only descriptive statistics provided were number of participants per cell and means. Without standard deviations, there is no way to determine how scores were distributed around the means, and therefore, no way to use the means to determine effect size. In the case of Rhenius and Deffner (1990) and Russo et al. (1989), ANOVAs were run on the data but neither F statistics, degrees of freedom, nor sums of squares were provided in the reports, making it impossible to calculate effect sizes for these studies. In the case of Stratman and Hamp-Lyons (1994), since no inferential statistical tests, such as t tests or ANOVAs, were run on the data, it was not possible to use other, more indirect, means of calculating the effect size.
2. It is important to note that the two studies that used background questionnaire information to assess proficiency were the two experiments reported in Sanz et al. (2009). These experiments were unique in that they sought to identify monolingually-raised English speakers with no previous exposure to or knowledge of Latin.

References

Abbott, M. (2006). ESL reading strategies: Differences in Arabic and Mandarin speaker test performance. *Language Learning*, *56*(4), 633–670.

Ahlum-Heath, M. E., & di Vesta, F. J. (1986). The effect of conscious controlled verbalization of a cognitive strategy on transfer in problem solving. *Memory and Cognition*, *14*(3), 281–285.

Allport, A. (1988). What concept of consciousness? In A. J. Marcel & E. Bisiach (Eds.), *Consciousness in contemporary science* (pp. 159–182). London: Clarendon Press.

Allwood, C. M. (1990). On the relation between justification of solution method and correctness of solution in statistical problem solving. *Scandinavian Journal of Psychology*, *31*(3), 181–190.

Alvermann, D. E. (1984). Second graders' strategic preferences while reading basal stories. *Journal of Educational Research*, *77*(3), 184–189.

Anderson, M. (1985). Some evidence on the effect of verbalization on process: A methodological note. *Journal of Accounting Research*, *23*, 843–852.

Anderson, N. J. (1991). Individual differences in strategy use in second language reading and testing. *Modern Language Journal*, *75*(4), 460–472.

Anderson, N. J., Bachman, L., Perkins, K., & Cohen, A. (1991). An exploratory study into the construct validity of a reading comprehension test: Triangulation of data sources. *Language Testing*, *8*(1), 41–66.

Anderson, U., & Wright, W. F. (1988). Expertise and the explanation effect. *Organizational Behavior and Human Decision Processes*, *42*, 250–269.

Baddeley, A. D. (1986). *Working memory*. Oxford: Clarendon Press.

Baumann, J. F., Jones, L. A., & Seifert Kessell, N. (1993). Using think alouds to enhance children's comprehension monitoring abilities. *Reading Teacher*, *47*(3), 184–193.

Beare, S. (2001). Differences in content generating and planning processes of adult L1 and L2 proficient writers. *Dissertation Abstracts International, A: The Humanities and Social Sciences*, *62*(2), 547–A.

Berardi-Coletta, B., Buyer, L. S., Dominowski, R. L., & Rellinger, E. R. (1995). Metacognition and problem solving: A process-oriented approach. *Journal of Experimental Psychology: Learning, Memory, and Cognition*, 21(1), 205–223.

Berg, H. P. (2002). Remediating cognitive perspective-taking in children with autism. Unpublished dissertation, Columbia University Teachers College, New York, NY.

Bernardi, L., Wdowczyk-Szulc, J., Valenti, C., Castoldi, S., Passino, C., Spadacini, G. et al. (2000). Effects of controlled breathing, mental activity, and mental stress with or without verbalization on heart rate variability. *Journal of the American College of Cardiology*, 35(6), 1462–1469.

Berry, D. C. (1983). Metacognitive experience and transfer of logical reasoning. *Quarterly Journal of Experimental Psychology*, 35A, 39–49.

Berry, D. C., & Broadbent, D. E. (1984). On the relationship between task performance and associated verbalizable knowledge. *Quarterly Journal of Experimental Psychology*, 36A, 209–231.

Biehal, G., & Chakravarti, D. (1989). The effects of concurrent verbalization on choice processing. *Journal of Marketing Research*, 26, 84–96.

Biggs, S. F., Rosman, A. J., & Sergenian, G. K. (1993). Methodological issues in judgment and decision-making research: Concurrent verbal protocol validity and simultaneous traces of process data. *Journal of Behavioral Decision Making*, 9, 234–248.

Block, E. L. (1986). The comprehension strategies of second language readers. *TESOL Quarterly*, 20, 463–494.

Bower, A. C., & King, W. L. (1967). The effect of number of irrelevant stimulus dimensions, verbalization, and sex on learning bi-conditional classification rules. *Psychonomic Science*, 8, 453–454.

Bowles, M. (2003). The effects of textual input enhancement on language learning: An online/offline study of fourth-semester Spanish students. In P. Kempchinsky & C. E. Piñeros (Eds.), *Theory, practice, and acquisition: Papers from the 6th Hispanic Linguistics Symposium and the 5th Conference on the Acquisition of Spanish and Portuguese* (pp. 395–411). Somerville, MA: Cascadilla Press.

Bowles, M. (2004). L2 glossing: To CALL or not to CALL. *Hispania*, 87(3), 543–555.

Bowles, M. (2008). Task type and reactivity of verbal reports in SLA: A first look at a task other than reading. *Studies in Second Language Acquisition*, 30(3), 359–387.

Bowles, M., & Leow, R. P. (2005). Reactivity and type of verbal report in SLA research methodology: Expanding the scope of investigation. *Studies in Second Language Acquisition*, 27(3), 415–440.

Bowles, M., Foote, R., Perpiñán, S., & Bhatt, R. (Eds.). (2008). *Selected proceedings of the 2007 Second Language Research Forum*. Somerville, MA: Cascadilla Proceedings Project.

Box, J. A. (2002). Guided writing in the early childhood classroom. *Reading Improvement*, 39(3), 111–113.

Bozarth, J. (1970). Verbal protocol patterns of college dormitory counselors. *Counselor Education and Supervision*, 10(1), 23–29.

Breetvelt, I. (1994). Relations between writing processes and text quality: When and how? *Cognition and Instruction*, *12*(2), 103–123.

Brehmer, B. (1974). Hypotheses about relations between scaled variables in the learning of probabilistic inference tasks. *Organizational Behavior and Human Performance*, *11*, 1–27.

Brehmer, B., Kuylenstierna, J., & Liljegren, J. E. (1974). Effects of functional form and cue validity on the subjects' hypotheses in probabilistic inference tasks. *Organizational Behavior and Human Performance*, *11*, 338–354.

Brinkman, J. A. (1993). Verbal protocol accuracy in fault diagnosis. *Ergonomics*, *36*(11), 1381–1397.

Brunk, L., Collister, G., Swift, C., & Stayton, S. (1958). A correlation study of two reasoning problems. *Journal of Experimental Psychology*, *55*, 236–241.

Carpenter, H., Jeon, K. S., MacGregor, D., & Mackey, A. (2006). Learners' interpretations of recasts. *Studies in Second Language Acquisition*, *28*(2), 209–236.

Carpenter, P. A., Just, M. A., & Schell, P. (1990). What one intelligence measures: A theoretical account of the processing in the Raven's Progressive Matrices Test. *Psychological Review*, *97*, 404–431.

Carr, T. H., & Curran, T. (1994). Cognitive factors in learning about structured sequences: Applications to syntax. *Studies in Second Language Acquisition*, *16*(2), 205–230.

Carrell, P. L. (1989). Metacognitive awareness and second language reading. *The Modern Language Journal*, *73*, 121–134.

Castro, C. D. (2004). The role of Tagalog in ESL writing: Clues from students' think-aloud protocols. *Philippine Journal of Linguistics*, *35*(2), Dec., 23–39.

Castro, D. (2005). Investigating the use of the native language in the process of writing in a second language: A qualitative approach. *Revista Virtual de Estudos da Linguagem, ReVEL*, *3*(5), n.p.

Cavalcanti, M. C., & Cohen, A. D. (1990). Comentarios em composições: Uma comparação dos pontos de vista do professor e do aluno [Comments on compositions: A comparison of the teacher's and student's points of view]. *Trabalhos em Lingüística Aplicada* (Vol. 15, pp. 7–23).

Chamot, A. U., & El Dinary, P. B. (1999). Children's learning strategies in language immersion classrooms. *The Modern Language Journal*, *83*(3), 319–338.

Chan, R. C., Hoosain, R., & Lee, T. M. (2002). Talking while performing a task: A better attentional performance in patients with closed head injury? *Journal of Clinical Experimental Neuropsychology*, *24*(5), 695–704.

Chenoweth, N. A., & Hayes, J. R. (2001). Fluency in writing: Generating text in L1 and L2. *Written Communication*, *18*(1), 80–98.

Clark, C. M. (1987). A note on method. Computer storage and manipulation of field notes and verbal protocols: Three cautions. *Anthropology and Education Quarterly*, *18*(1), 56–58.

Cohen, A. D. (1986). Mentalistic measures in reading strategy research: Some recent findings. *English for Specific Purposes*, *5*(2), 131–145.

Cohen, A. D. (1987). Recent uses of mentalistic data in reading strategy research. *Revista de Documentação de Estudos em Lingüística Teorica e Aplicada, 3*(1), 57–84.

Cohen, A. D. (1998a). Contrastive analysis of speech acts: What do we do with the research findings? *Studia Anglica Posnaniensia, 33,* 81–92.

Cohen, A. D. (1998b). *Strategies in learning and using a second language.* New York: Longman.

Cohen, A. D. (2000). Exploring strategies in test taking: Fine-tuning verbal reports from respondents. In G. Ekbatani & H. Pierson (Eds.), *Learner-directed assessment in ESL* (pp. 127–150). Mahwah, NJ: Lawrence Erlbaum Associates.

Cohen, A. D., & Cavalcanti, M. C. (1987). Viewing feedback on compositions from the teacher's and the student's perspective. *ESPecialist, 16*(Apr.), 13–28.

Cohen, A. D., & Hosenfeld, C. (1981). Some uses of mentalistic data in second language research. *Language Learning, 31*(2), 285–313.

Cohen, A. D., & Olshtain, E. (1993). The production of speech acts by EFL learners. *TESOL Quarterly, 27,* 33–56.

Cohen, A. D., & Upton, T. A. (2007). 'I want to go back to the text': Response strategies on the reading subtest of the new TOEFL. *Language Testing, 24*(2), 209–250.

Cohen, J. (1988). *Statistical power analysis for the behavioral sciences.* Hillsdale, NJ: Lawrence Erlbaum Associates.

Cooper, H., & Hedges, L. (Eds.). (1994). *The handbook of research synthesis.* New York: Russell Sage Foundation.

Corder, S. P. (1973). The elicitation of interlanguage. In J. Svartik (Ed.), *Errata: Papers in error analysis* (pp. 36–48). Lund: CKW Geerup.

Cushman, D. (2002). From scribbles to stories. *Instructor, 111*(5), 32–33.

Davis, J., & Bistodeau, L. (1993). How do L1 and L2 reading differ? Evidence from think aloud protocols. *The Modern Language Journal, 77,* 459–472.

Davis, J. H., Carey, M. H., Foxman, P. N., & Tarr, D. B. (1968). Verbalization, experimenter presence, and problem solving. *Journal of Personality and Social Psychology, 8,* 299–302.

Deffner, G. (1984). *Lautes Denken: Untersuchung zur Qualität eines Datenerhebungsverfahrens* [*Thinking aloud: An investigation into the quality of a data collection procedure*]. Frankfurt: Lang.

Deffner, G. (1989). Interaktion zwischen Lautem Denken, Bearbeitungsstrategien und Aufgabenmerkmalen? Eine experimentelle Prüfung des Modells von Ericsson und Simon [Interaction of thinking aloud, solution strategies, and task characteristics? An experimental test of the Ericsson and Simon model]. *Sprache & Kognition, 8,* 98–111.

de Larios, R., Marin, J., & Murphy, L. (2001). A temporal analysis of formulation processes in L1 and L2 writing. *Language Learning, 51*(3), 497–538.

Dickson, J., McLennan, J., & Omodei, M. M. (2000). Effects of concurrent verbalization on a time-critical, dynamic decision-making task. *The Journal of General Psychology, 127*(2), 217–228.

Dubin, R., & Taveggia, T. (1968). *The teaching-learning paradox: A comparative analysis of college teaching methods.* Eugene, OR: University of Oregon Press.

Durst, R. K. (1987). Cognitive and linguistic demands of analytic writing. *Research in the Teaching of English, 21*(4), 347–376.

Earthman, E. A. (1992). Creating the virtual work: Readers' processes in understanding literary texts. *Research in the Teaching of English, 26*(4), 351–384.

Ellis, R. (2001). Introduction: Investigating form-focused instruction. *Language Learning, 51*(Suppl. 1), 1–46.

Ellis, R. (2004). The definition and measurement of L2 explicit knowledge. *Language Learning, 54*(2), 227–275.

Ellis, R. (2005). Measuring implicit and explicit knowledge of a second language: A psychometric study. *Studies in Second Language Acquisition, 27,* 141–172.

El Mortaji, L. (2001). Writing ability and strategies in two discourse types: A cognitive study of multilingual Moroccan university students writing in Arabic (L1) and English (L3). *Dissertation Abstracts International, C: Worldwide, 62*(4), 499–C.

Enkvist, I. (1995). Intellectual and linguistic processes in foreign language students: Students' development during their first year of Spanish at a Swedish university. In *Studies of Higher Education and Research.* Washington, DC: ERIC Clearinghouse.

Ericsson, K. A. (2002). Towards a procedure for eliciting verbal expression of non-verbal experience without reactivity: Interpreting the verbal overshadowing effect within the theoretical framework for protocol analysis. *Applied Cognitive Psychology, 16,* 981–987.

Ericsson, K. A., & Simon, H. A. (1984). *Protocol analysis: Verbal reports as data.* Cambridge, MA: MIT.

Ericsson, K. A., & Simon, H. A. (1993). *Protocol analysis: Verbal reports as data* (rev. ed.). Cambridge, MA: MIT.

Evans, J. S. B. T., Barston, J. L., & Pollard, P. (1983). On the conflict between logic and belief in syllogistic reasoning. *Memory & Cognition, 11,* 295–306.

Ewert, P. H., & Lambert, J. F. (1932). Part II: The effect of verbal instructions upon the formation of a concept. *Journal of General Psychology, 6,* 400–413.

Færch, C., & Kasper, G. (1986). One learner – two languages: Investigating types of interlanguage knowledge. In J. House & S. Blum-Kulka (Eds.), *Interlingual and intercultural communication* (pp. 211–227). Tubingen: Gunter Narr.

Farrington-Flint, L., & Wood, C. (2007). The role of lexical analogies in beginning reading: Insights from children's self-reports. *Journal of Educational Psychology, 99*(2), 326–338.

Fehrenbach, C. R. (1991). Gifted/average readers: Do they use the same reading strategies? *Gifted Child Quarterly*, *35*(3), 125–127.

Félix-Brasdefer, J. (2004). Interlanguage refusals: Linguistic politeness and length of residence in the target community. *Language Learning*, *54*(4), 587–653.

Félix-Brasdefer, J. (2008). Perceptions of refusals to invitations: Exploring the minds of foreign language learners. *Language Awareness*, *17*(3), 195–211.

Fidler, E. J. (1983). The reliability and validity of concurrent, retrospective, and interpretive verbal reports: An experimental study. In P. Humphreys, O. Svenson, & A. Vari (Eds.), *Analyzing and aiding decision processes* (pp. 429–440). Amsterdam: Elsevier Science Publishing Company.

Folger, T. L. (2001). Readers' parallel text construction while talking and thinking about the reading process. *Dissertation Abstracts International, A: The Humanities and Social Sciences*, *62*(4), 1329–A.

Fowler, L. P. (1997). Clinical reasoning strategies used during care planning. *Clinical Nursing Research*, *6*(4), 349–361.

Fraser, J. (1993). Public accounts: Using verbal protocols to investigate community translation. *Applied Linguistics*, *14*(4), 325–343.

Fresch, M. J., Wheaton, A., & Zutell, J. B. (1998). Thinking aloud during spelling word sorts. *National Reading Conference Yearbook*, *47*, 285–294.

Friedman, P., & Mulhern, S.T. (1976). Relationship of clinician feedback to child-initiated verbalization during language training. *Journal of Communication Disorders*, *9*(4), 289–299.

Gagné, R. H., & Smith, E. C. (1962). A study of the effects of verbalization on problem solving. *Journal of Experimental Psychology*, *63*, 12–18.

Gass, S., & Mackey, A. (2000). *Stimulated recall methodology in second language research*. Mahwah, NJ: Lawrence Erlbaum.

Gavin, C. A. (1989). The strategies of native and limited English proficient test-takers as revealed by think-aloud protocols. *Dissertation Abstracts International, A: The Humanities and Social Sciences*, *50*(3), 640–A.

Gordon, C. J. (1990). Modeling an expository text structure strategy in think alouds. *Reading Horizons*, *31*(2), 149–167.

Green, A. J. F. (1998). *Using verbal protocols in language testing research: A handbook*. Cambridge: Cambridge University Press.

Greenwood, J., & King, M. (1995). Some surprising similarities in the clinical reasoning of expert and novice orthopaedic nurses: Report of a study using verbal protocols and protocol analysis. *Journal of Advanced Nursing*, *22*(5), 907–913.

Hafner, J. (1957). Influence of verbalization on problem solving. *Psychological Reports*, *3*, 360.

Hagafors, R., & Brehmer, B. (1983). Does having to justify one's judgments change the nature of the judgment process? *Organizational Behavior and Human Performance*, *31*, 223–232.

Harmon, J. M. (2000). Assessing and supporting independent word learning strategies of middle school students. *Journal of Adolescent and Adult Literacy*, *43*(6), 518–527.

Hatasa, Y. A., & Soeda, E. (2000). Writing strategies revisited: A case of non-cognate L2 writers. In B. Swierzbin, F. Morris, M. Anderson, C. A. Klee, & E. Tarone (Eds.), *Social and cognitive factors in second language acquisition: Selected proceedings of the 1999 Second Language Research Forum* (pp. 375–396). Somerville, MA: Cascadilla.

Hedges, L., Shymansky, J., & Woodworth, G. (1989). *A practical guide to modern methods of meta-analysis*. Washington, DC: National Science Teachers Association.

Herwig, A. (2003). Plurilingual lexical organisation: Evidence from lexical processing in L1–L2–L3–L4 translation. In J. Cenoz, B. Hufeisen, & U. Jessner (Eds.), *Cross linguistic influence in third language acquisition: Psychological perspectives* (pp. 115–137). Clevedon, England: Multilingual Matters.

Hosenfeld, C. (1976). Learning about learning: Discovering our students' strategies. *Foreign Language Annals, 9*, 117–129.

Hosenfeld, C. (1977). A preliminary investigation of the reading strategies of successful and nonsuccessful second language learners. *System, 5*(2), 110–123.

Hosenfeld, C. (1979). Cindy: A learner in today's foreign language classroom. In W. Borne (Ed.), *The foreign language learner in today's classroom environment* (pp. 53–75). Montpelier, VT: Northwest Conference on the Teaching of Foreign Languages.

Hosenfeld, C. (1984). Case studies of ninth grade readers. In J. C. Alderson & A. H. Urquhart (Eds.), *Reading in a foreign language* (pp. 231–249). London: Longman.

Hu, G. (2002). Psychological constraints on the utility of metalinguistic knowledge in second language production. *Studies in Second Language Acquisition, 24*, 347–386.

Hughes, J., & Parkes, S. (2003). Trends in the use of verbal protocol analysis in software engineering research. *Behaviour & Information Technology, 22*(2), 127–141.

Hyona, J., & Nurminen, A.-M. (2006). Do adult readers know how they read? Evidence from eye movement patterns and verbal reports. *British Journal of Psychology, 97*(1), 31–50.

Jaaskelainen, R. (2000). Focus on methodology in think-aloud studies on translating. In S. Tirkkonen Condit & R. Jaaskelainen (Eds.), *Tapping and mapping the processes of translation and interpreting: Outlooks on empirical research* (pp. 71–82). Amsterdam: John Benjamins.

Jannausch, U. H. (2002). A case study of native speakers of English composing in German as a foreign language. *Dissertation Abstracts International, A: The Humanities and Social Sciences, 62*(12), 4144–A.

Jimenez, R. T., Garcia, G. E., & Pearson, P. D. (1996). The reading strategies of bilingual Latina/o students who are successful English readers: Opportunities and obstacles. *Reading Research Quarterly, 31*(1), 90–112.

Jourdenais, R. (2001). Cognition, instruction, and protocol analysis. In

P. Robinson (Ed.), *Cognition and second language instruction.* Cambridge: Cambridge University Press.

Karsenty, L. (2001). Adapting verbal protocol methods to investigate speech systems use. *Applied Ergonomics, 32*(1), 15–22.

Kasper, G. (1999). Data collection in pragmatics research. *University of Hawai'i Working Papers in ESL, 18*(1), 71–107.

Kasper, G., & Blum-Kulka, S. (1993). *Interlanguage pragmatics.* New York: Oxford University Press.

Kasper, G., & Rose, K. (2002). *Pragmatic development in a second language.* Malden, MA: Blackwell.

Katona, G. (1940). *Organizing and memorizing.* New York: Columbia University Press.

Keck, C. M., Iberri-Shea, G., Tracy-Ventura, N., & Wa-Mbaleka, S. (2006). Investigating the empirical link between task-based interaction and acquisition: A quantitative meta-analysis. In J. M. Norris & L. Ortega (Eds.), *Synthesizing research on language learning and teaching.* Amsterdam: John Benjamins.

Kern, R. G. (1994). The role of mental translation in second language reading. *Studies in Second Language Acquisition, 16*(4), 441–461.

Knoblich, G., & Rhenius, D. (1995). Zur Reaktivität Lauten Denkens beim komplexen Problemlösen [The reactivity of thinking aloud during complex problem solving]. *Zeitschrift für Experimentelle Psychologie, 42,* 419–454.

Ko, M. H. (2005). Glosses, comprehension, and strategy use. *Reading in a Foreign Language, 17*(2), 125–143.

Krippendorf, K. (2003). *Content analysis: An introduction to its methodology.* London: Sage.

Lass, U., Klettke, W., Lüer, G., & Ruhlender, P. (1991). Does thinking aloud influence the structure of cognitive processes? In R. Schmid & D. Zambarbieri (Eds.), *Oculomotor control and cognitive processes* (pp. 385–396). Amsterdam: North-Holland Publishing Co.

Lee, S.-K., & Huang, H.-T. (2008). Visual input enhancement and grammar learning: A meta-analytic review. *Studies in Second Language Acquisition, 30*(3), 307–331.

Leow, R. P. (1997a). Attention, awareness, and foreign language behavior. *Language Learning, 47*(3), 467–505.

Leow, R. P. (1997b). The effects of input enhancement and text length on adult L2 readers' comprehension and intake in second language acquisition. *Applied Language Learning, 8*(2), 151–182.

Leow, R. P. (1998a). The effects of amount and type of exposure on adult learners' L2 development in SLA. *Modern Language Journal, 82*(1), 49–68.

Leow, R. P. (1998b). Toward operationalizing the process of attention in SLA: Evidence for Tomlin and Villa's (1994) fine-grained analysis of attention. *Applied Psycholinguistics, 19*(1), 133–159.

Leow, R. P. (1999). The role of attention in second/foreign language classroom research: Methodological issues. In F. M.-G. J. Gutiérrez-Rexach

(Ed.), *Advances in Hispanic Linguistics: Papers from the 2nd Hispanic Linguistics Symposium* (pp. 60–71). Somerville, MA: Cascadilla.

Leow, R. P. (2000). A study of the role of awareness in foreign language behavior: Aware versus unaware learners. *Studies in Second Language Acquisition, 22*(4), 557–584.

Leow, R. P. (2001a). Attention, awareness, and foreign language behavior. *Language Learning, 51*(Suppl. 1), 113–155.

Leow, R. P. (2001b). Do learners notice enhanced forms while interacting with the L2? An online and offline study of the role of written input enhancement in L2 reading. *Hispania, 84*(3), 496–509.

Leow, R. P., & Bowles, M. (2005). Attention and awareness in SLA. In C. Sanz (Ed.), *Mind and context in adult second language acquisition: Methods, theory, and practice* (pp. 179–203). Washington, DC: Georgetown University Press.

Leow, R. P., & Morgan-Short, K. (2004). To think aloud or not to think aloud: The issue of reactivity in SLA research methodology. *Studies in Second Language Acquisition, 26*(1), 35–57.

Light, R., & Pillemer, D. (1984). *Summing up: The science of reviewing research*. Cambridge, MA: Harvard University Press.

Lipsey, M. W., & Wilson, D. B. (2001). *Practical meta-analysis*. Thousand Oaks, CA: Sage Publications.

Liu, J. (2006). Measuring interlanguage pragmatic knowledge of Chinese EFL learners. *Foreign Language Teaching and Research, 38*(4), 259–265.

Lomicka, L. (1998). To gloss or not to gloss: An investigation of reading comprehension online. *Language Learning & Technology, 1*, 41–50.

Long, M. (1996). The role of the linguistic environment in second language acquisition. In W. C. Ritchie & T. K. Bhatia (Eds.), *Handbook of second language acquisition* (pp. 413–468). San Diego, CA: Academic Press.

McGeorge, P., & Burton, A. M. (1989). The effects of concurrent verbalization on performance in a dynamic systems task. *British Journal of Psychology, 80*, 455–465.

McGuire, K. L., & Yewchuk, C. R. (1996). Use of metacognitive reading strategies by gifted learning disabled students: An exploratory study. *Journal for the Education of the Gifted, 19*(3), 293–314.

Mackey, A. (Ed.). (2007). *Conversational interaction in second language acquisition*. Oxford: Oxford University Press.

Mackey, A., & Gass, S. (2005). *Second language research: Methodology and design*. Mahwah, NJ: Lawrence Erlbaum.

Mackey, A., & Goo, J. (2007). Interaction research in SLA: A meta-analysis and research synthesis. In A. Mackey (Ed.), *Conversational interaction in second language acquisition* (pp. 407–452). Oxford: Oxford University Press.

Mackey, A., Gass, S., & McDonough, K. (2000). How do learners perceive interactional feedback? *Studies in Second Language Acquisition, 22*(4), 471–497.

Maeng, U. (2005). A comparative study of reading strategies in L1 and L2:

Case study of five Korean graduate students. *Ohak Yon'gu/Language Research, 41*(2), June, 457–490.

Markee, N. (2005). Conversation analysis for second language acquisition. In E. Hinkel (Ed.), *Handbook of research in second language teaching and learning* (pp. 355–374). Mahwah, NJ: Lawrence Erlbaum.

Marks, M. R. (1951). Problem solving as a function of the situation. *Journal of Experimental Psychology, 41,* 74–80.

Masgoret, A. M., & Gardner, R. C. (2003). Attitude, motivation, and second language learning: A meta-analysis of studies conducted by Gardner and associates. *Language Learning, 53*(123–163).

Mathews, R. C., Buss, R. R., Stanley, W. B., Blanchard-Fields, F., Cho, J. R., & Druhan, B. (1989). Role of implicit and explicit processes in learning from examples: A synergistic effect. *Journal of Experimental Psychology: Learning, Memory, and Cognition, 15,* 1083–1100.

Midanik, L. T., & Hines, A. M. (1991). "Unstandard" ways of answering standard questions: Protocol analysis in alcohol survey research. *Drug and Alcohol Dependence, 27,* 245–252.

Nabei, T., & Swain, M. (2002). Learner awareness of recasts in classroom interaction: A case study of an adult EFL student's second language learning. *Language Awareness, 11,* 43–63.

Nassaji, H. (2006). The relationship between depth of vocabulary knowledge and L2 learners' lexical inferencing strategy use and success. *The Modern Language Journal, 90*(3), 387–401.

Nevo, N. (1989). Test-taking strategies on a multiple-choice test of reading comprehension. *Language Testing, 6*(2), 199–215.

Nisbett, R. E., & Wilson, T. D. (1977). Telling more than we can know: Verbal reports on mental processes. *Psychological Review, 84,* 231–259.

Nissen, M., & Bullemer, P. (1987). Attentional requirements of learning: Evidence from performance measures. *Cognitive Psychology, 19,* 1–32.

Nist, S. L., & Kirby, K. (1986). Teaching comprehension and study strategies through modeling and thinking aloud. *Reading Research and Instruction, 25*(4), 254–264.

Norris, J. M., & Ortega, L. (2000). Effectiveness of L2 instruction: A research synthesis and quantitative meta-analysis. *Language Learning, 50,* 417–528.

Norris, J. M., & Ortega, L. (Eds.). (2006). *Synthesizing research on language learning and teaching.* Amsterdam: John Benjamins.

Norris, S. P. (1990). Effect of eliciting verbal reports of thinking on critical thinking test performance. *Journal of Educational Measurement, 27,* 41–58.

Norris, S. P. (1992). A demonstration of the use of verbal reports of thinking in multiple-choice critical thinking test design. *The Alberta Journal of Educational Research, 38*(3), 155–176.

Payne, J. W., Braunstein, M. L., & Carroll, J. S. (1978). Exploring predecisional behavior: An alternative approach to decision research. *Organizational Behavior and Human Performance, 22,* 17–44.

Philp, J. (2003). Nonnative speakers' noticing of recasts in NS-NNS interaction. *Studies in Second Language Acquisition, 25,* 99–126.

Piolat, A., & Olive, T. (2000). Comment étudier le coût et le déroulement de la rédaction de textes? La méthode de la triple tâche: Un bilan méthodologique [How can the process and cost of writing be studied?: The triple task method, a methodological review]. *L'Annee Psychologique, 465,* 465–502.

Poehner, M. (2007). Beyond the test: L2 dynamic assessment and the transcendence of mediated learning. *The Modern Language Journal, 91*(3), 323–340.

Polio, C., & Wang, J. (in review). Another look at the reactivity of concurrent verbal protocols in second language reading research: A replication of Leow and Morgan-Short (2004). *Studies in Second Language Acquisition.*

Polio, C., Gass, S., & Chapin, L. (2006). Using stimulated recall to investigate native speaker perceptions in native-nonnative speaker interaction. *Studies in Second Language Acquisition, 28*(2), 237–267.

Poulisse, N. (1990). *The use of compensatory strategies by Dutch learners of English.* Dordrecht: Foris.

Poulisse, N., Bongaerts, T., & Kellerman, E. (1987). The use of retrospective verbal reports in the analysis of compensatory strategies. In C. Faersch & G. Kasper (Eds.), *Introspection in second language research* (pp. 213–229). Clevedon: Multilingual Matters.

Pressley, M., & Afflerbach, P. (1995). *Verbal protocols of reading: The nature of constructively responsive reading.* Hillsdale, NJ: Erlbaum.

Pritchard, R. (1990). The effects of cultural schemata on reading processing strategies. *Reading Research Quarterly, 25,* 273–295.

Qi, D., & Lapkin, S. (2001). Exploring the role of noticing in a three-stage second language writing task. *Journal of Second Language Writing, 10,* 277–303.

Rhenius, D., & Deffner, G. (1990). Evaluation of concurrent thinking aloud using eye-tracking data. In M. E. Wiklund (Ed.), *Proceedings of the Human Factors Society 34th Annual Meeting.* Santa Monica, CA: Human Factors Society.

Rhenius, D., & Heydemann, M. (1984). Lautes Denken beim Bearbeiten von RAVEN-Aufgaben [Thinking aloud while processing Raven's Matrices]. *Zeitschrift für experimentelle und angewandte Psychologie, 31,* 308–327.

Robertson, B. (1995). Why think along? Using "think alouds" in the classroom. *State of Reading, 2*(1), 19–22.

Robinson, K. M. (2001). The validity of verbal reports in children's subtraction. *Journal of Educational Psychology, 93,* 211–222.

Robinson, M. (1991). Introspective methodology in interlanguage pragmatics research. In *Pragmatics of Japanese as native and target language* (pp. 29–84). Honolulu: University of Hawai'i Second Language Teaching and Curriculum Center.

Robinson, P. (1995). Attention, memory, and the "noticing" hypothesis. *Language Learning, 45*(2), 283–331.

Robinson, P. (1996). *Consciousness, rules, and instructed second language acquisition.* New York: Peter Lang Publishing, Inc.

Ronowicz, E., Hehir, J., Kaimi, T., Kojima, K., & Lee, D.-S. (2005). Translator's frequent lexis store and dictionary use as factors in SLT comprehension and translation speed: A comparative study of professional, paraprofessional and novice translators. *Meta, 50*(2), 580–596.

Rosa, E. (1999). A cognitive approach to task-based research: Explicitness, awareness and L2 development. *Dissertation Abstracts International, A: The Humanities and Social Sciences, 60*(12), 4405–A.

Rosa, E., & Leow, R. P. (2004a). Awareness, different learning conditions, and L2 development. *Applied Psycholinguistics, 25*(2), 269–292.

Rosa, E., & Leow, R. P. (2004b). Computerized task-based exposure, explicitness, type of feedback, and Spanish L2 development. *The Modern Language Journal, 88*(2), 192–216.

Rosa, E., & O'Neill, M. (1999). Explicitness, intake, and the issue of awareness. *Studies in Second Language Acquisition, 21*(4), 511–556.

Rosenshine, B., & Meister, C. (1992). The use of scaffolds for teaching higher-level cognitive strategies. *Educational Leadership, 49*(7), 26–33.

Rosenthal, M. C. (1994). The fugitive literature. In H. Cooper & L. Hedges (Eds.), *Handbook of research synthesis* (pp. 85–94). New York: Russell Sage Foundation.

Rosenthal, R. (1991). *Meta-analytic procedures for social research.* Newbury Park, CA: Sage.

Rossomondo, A. E. (2007). The role of lexical temporal indicators and text interaction format in the incidental acquisition of the Spanish future tense. *Studies in Second Language Acquisition, 29*(1), 39–66.

Rott, S. (2005). Processing glosses: A qualitative exploration of how form-meaning connections are established and strengthened. *Reading in a Foreign Language, 17*(2), 95–124.

Russell, J., & Spada, N. (2006). The effectiveness of corrective feedback for the acquisition of L2 grammar: A meta-analysis of the research. In J. M. Norris & L. Ortega (Eds.), *Synthesizing research on language learning and teaching* (pp. 133–164). Amsterdam: John Benjamins.

Russo, J. E., Johnson, E. J., & Stephens, D. L. (1989). The validity of verbal protocols. *Memory & Cognition, 17*, 759–769.

Sachs, R., & Polio, C. (2007). Learners' uses of two types of written feedback on an L2 writing revision task. *Studies in Second Language Acquisition, 29*(1), 67–100.

Sachs, R., & Suh, B. R. (2007). Textually enhanced recasts, learner awareness, and L2 outcomes in synchronous computer-mediated interaction. In A. Mackey (Ed.), *Conversational interaction in second language acquisition: A collection of empirical studies* (pp. 197–227). Oxford: Oxford University Press.

Sanz, C., Lin, H.-J., Lado, B., Bowden, H. W., & Stafford, C. A. (2009). Concurrent verbalizations, pedagogical conditions, and reactivity: Two CALL studies. *Language Learning, 59*(1), 33–71.

Scardamalia, M. (1984). Teachability of reflective processes in written composition. *Cognitive Science: A Multidisciplinary Journal of Artificial Intelligence, 8*(2), 173–190.

Schmid, R., & Zambarbieri, D. (Eds.). (1991). *Oculomotor control and cognitive processes.* Amsterdam: North-Holland Publishing.

Schmidt, R. (1990). The role of consciousness in second language learning. *Applied Linguistics, 11*(2), 129–158.

Schmidt, R. (1993). Awareness and second language acquisition. *Annual Review of Applied Linguistics, 13*, 206–226.

Schmidt, R. (1994). Deconstructing consciousness in search of useful definitions for applied linguistics. *AILA Review, 11*, 11–26.

Schmidt, R. (1995). Consciousness and foreign language learning: A tutorial on the role of attention and awareness in learning. In R. W. Schmidt (Ed.), *Attention and awareness in foreign language learning.* Honolulu, HI: University of Hawai'i.

Schmidt, R. (2001). Attention. In P. Robinson (Ed.), *Cognition and second language instruction* (pp. 3–32). Cambridge: Cambridge University Press.

Schooler, J. W., Ohlsson, S., & Brooks, K. (1993). Thoughts beyond words: When language overshadows insight. *Journal of Experimental Psychology, 122*(2), 166–183.

Seguinot, C. (1996). Some thoughts about think-aloud protocols. *Target, 8*(1), 75–95.

Selinker, L. (1972). Interlanguage. *International Review of Applied Linguistics, 10*, 209–231.

Seng, G. H., & Hashim, F. (2006). Use of L1 in L2 reading comprehension among tertiary ESL learners. *Reading in a Foreign Language, 18*(1), 29–54.

Shlesinger, M. (2000). Interpreting as a cognitive process: How can we know what really happens? In S. Tirkkonen Condit & R. Jaaskelainen (Eds.), *Tapping and mapping the processes of translation and interpreting: Outlooks on empirical research* (pp. 3–15). Amsterdam: John Benjamins.

Short, E. J., Schatschneider, C., Cuddy, C. L., Evans, S. W., Dellick, D. M., & Basili, L. A. (1991). The effect of thinking aloud on the problem solving performance of bright, average, learning disabled, and developmentally handicapped students. *Contemporary Educational Psychology, 16*, 139–153.

Smagorinsky, P. (2001). Rethinking protocol analysis from a cultural perspective. *Annual Review of Applied Linguistics, 21*, 233–245.

Stanley, W. B., Mathews, R. C., Buss, R. R., & Kotler-Cope, S. (1989). Insight without awareness: On the interaction of verbalization, instruction, and practice in a simulated process control task. *The Quarterly Journal of Experimental Psychology, 41A*, 553–577.

Steinberg, I., Bohning, G., & Chowning, F. (1991). Comprehension monitoring strategies of nonproficient college readers. *Reading Research and Instruction, 30*(3), 63–75.

Stinessen, L. (1985). The influence of verbalization on problem solving. *Scandinavian Journal of Psychology, 26*, 342–347.

Storey, P. (1997). Examining the test-taking process: A cognitive perspective on the discourse cloze test. *Language Testing, 14*(2), 214–231.

Stratman, J. F., & Hamp-Lyons, L. (1994). Reactivity in concurrent think-aloud protocols. In P. Smagorinsky (Ed.), *Speaking about writing: Reflections on research methodology* (pp. 89–112). London: Sage.

Swain, M. (2006a). Languaging, agency and collaboration in advanced language proficiency. In H. Byrnes (Ed.), *Advanced language learning: The contribution of Halliday and Vygotsky* (pp. 95–108). London: Continuum.

Swain, M. (2006b). Verbal protocols: What does it mean for research to use speaking as a data collection tool? In M. Chalhoub-Deville, C. Chapelle, & P. Duff (Eds.), *Inference and generalizability in applied linguistics: Multiple perspectives* (pp. 97–113). Amsterdam: John Benjamins.

Taguchi, N. (2008). Pragmatic comprehension in Japanese as a foreign language. *The Modern Language Journal, 92*(4), 558–576.

Thomas, M. (2006). Research synthesis and historiography: The case of assessment of second language proficiency. In J. M. Norris & L. Ortega (Eds.), *Synthesizing research on language learning and teaching* (pp. 279–298). Amsterdam: Benjamins.

Tomlin, R. S., & Villa, V. (1994). Attention in cognitive science and second language acquisition. *Studies in Second Language Acquisition, 16*(2), 183–203.

Upton, T. A., & Lee Thompson, L. C. (2001). The role of the first language in second language reading. *Studies in Second Language Acquisition, 23*(4), 469–495.

Uzawa, K. (1996). Second language learners' processes of L1 writing, L2 writing, and translation from L1 into L2. *Journal of Second Language Writing, 5*(3), 271–294.

Vygotsky, L. (1987). *The collected works of L.S. Vygotsky* (Vol. I.). New York: Plenum.

Wade, S. E. (1990). Using think alouds to assess comprehension. *Reading Teacher, 43*(7), 442–451.

Walczyk, J., Marsiglia, C. S., Bryan, K. S., & Naquin, P. J. (2001). Overcoming inefficient reading skills. *Journal of Educational Psychology, 93*(4), 750–757.

Walters, F. S. (2007). A conversation-analytic hermeneutic rating protocol to assess L2 oral pragmatic competence. *Language Testing, 24*(2), 155–183.

Wang, H. (2001). Designing short answer reading comprehension questions for a college English test in China. *Dissertation Abstracts International, A: The Humanities and Social Sciences, 62*(5), 1819–A.

Wang, W., & Wen, Q. (2002). L1 use in the L2 composing process: An exploratory study of 16 Chinese EFL writers. *Journal of Second Language Writing, 11*(3), 225–246.

Warren, J. (1996). How students pick the right answer: A "think aloud" study of the French CAT. *Occasional Papers Applied Linguistics Association of Australia, 15*, 79–94.

Weber, R. P. (1990). *Basic content analysis*. London: Sage.

Wijgh, I. F. (1996). A communicative test in analysis: Strategies in reading authentic texts. In A. Cumming & R. Berwick (Eds.), *Validation in Language Testing* (pp. 154–170). Clevedon: Multilingual Matters.

Wilder, L., & Harvey, D. J. (1971). Overt and covert verbalization and problem solving. *Speech Monographs, 38*, 171–176.

Wilhelm, J. (2001). Getting kids into the reading game: You gotta know the rules. *Voices from the Middle, 8*(4), 25–36.

Williams, A. M., & Davids, K. (1997). Assessing cue usage in performance contexts: A comparison between eye-movement and concurrent verbal report methods. *Behavior Research Method, Instruments, & Computers, 29*(3), 364–375.

Wilson, T. D., & Schooler, J. W. (1991). Thinking too much: Introspection can reduce the quality of preferences and decisions. *Journal of Personality and Social Psychology, 60*, 181–192.

Witte, S. P., & Cherry, R. D. (1994). Think-aloud protocols, protocol analysis, and research design: An exploration of the influence of writing tasks on writing processes. In P. Smagorinsky (Ed.), *Speaking about writing: Reflections on research methodology* (pp. 20–54). London: Sage.

Woodfield, H. (2008). Problematising discourse completion tasks: Voices from verbal report. *Evaluation and Research in Education, 21*(1), 43–69.

Yamashita, J. (2002). Reading strategies in L1 and L2: Comparison of four groups of readers with different reading ability in L1 and L2. *ITL, Review of Applied Linguistics, 135–136*, 1–35.

Yang, Y.-F. (2006). Reading strategies or comprehension monitoring strategies? *Reading Psychology, 27*(4), 313–343.

Yoshida, M. (2008). Think-aloud protocols and type of reading task: The issue of reactivity in L2 reading research. In M. Bowles, R. Foote, S. Perpiñán, & R. Bhatt (Eds.), *Selected proceedings of the 2007 Second Language Research Forum* (pp. 199–209). Somerville, MA: Cascadilla Proceedings Project.

Zellermayer, M., & Cohen, J. (1996). Varying paths for learning to revise. *Instructional Science, 24*(3), 177–195.

Index

Abbott, M. 8
addition 54–5, 57, 60, 62–4
Afflerbach, P. 8
Ahlum-Heath, M. E. 24–6, 41, 46
Allport, A. 127–8
Allwood, C. M. 24, 39, 40–2, 46
Alvermann, D. E. 6
anagrams 17–19, 23, 54–7, 60, 81
analogies 30, 35–6, 56, 60, 82, 147
Anderson, M. 5, 15–16, 19, 20
Anderson, N. J. 7, 128
Anderson, U. 37
artificial grammar 44–5, 56–7, 60

Bachman, L. 7
Barston, J. L. 43–4
Basili, L. A. 30, 57, 93, 142
Baumann, J. F. 6
Beare, S. 9
Berardi-Coletta, B. 24, 41, 46–8
Berg, H. P. 6
Bernardi, L. 6
Berry, D. C. 30–1, 34, 36, 38, 46, 61
Bhatt, R. 86
Biehal, G. 5, 43–5
Biggs, S. F. 15, 17, 19
Bistodeau, L. 8–9
Blanchard-Fields, F. 31, 43–5, 56–7, 83, 141, 146
Block, E. L. 128
Blum-Kulka, S. 8, 10
Bohning, G. 128
Bongaerts, T. 10
Bowden, H. W. 72, 75, 80, 87–8, 94, 103, 109, 115–18, 120, 142

Bower, A. C. 29, 30, 46
Bowles, M. 9, 11, 12, 13–14, 67, 69, 70–1, 74–5, 86, 88, 92–3, 113–14, 116–18, 120, 124–6, 141–42, 144, 146–7
Box, J. A. 7
Bozarth, J. 5
brand decision 44–5, 60
Braunstein, M. L. 14
Breetvelt, I. 6
Brehmer, B. 30, 37, 39, 43–4, 52–3, 61
Brinkman, J. A. 5, 15, 17, 19
Broadbent, D. E. 30–1, 34, 38, 46, 61
Brooks, K. 24, 31, 36–7, 46
Brunk, L. 5, 24–5, 29, 41, 47, 50, 51
Bryan, K. S. 6
Bullemer, P. 127
Burton, A. M. 34, 46, 61
Buss, R. R. 31, 44, 57, 141
Buyer, L. S. 24, 41, 46–8

Carey, M. H. 30, 32, 46
Carpenter, H. 10
Carpenter, P. A. 24–6, 29, 41, 46, 62
Carr, T. H. 127
Carrell, P. L. 8
Carroll, J. S. 14
Castoldi, S. 6
Castro, C. D. 9
Castro, D. 9
Cavalcanti, M. C. 8
Chakravarti, D. 4, 43–5
Chamot, A. U. 8–9

Chan, R. C. 6
Chapin, L. 10
Chenoweth, N. A. 9
Cherry, R. D. 81
Cho, J. R. 31, 43–5, 56–7, 83, 141, 146
Chowning, F. 128
Clark, C. M. 5
classification of verbal reports 12
Cohen, A. D. 6–10
Cohen, J. 82
Collister, G. 5, 24–5, 29, 41, 47, 50, 51
concurrent (report) 1, 5, 8, 10–11, 13–15, 19, 23, 26–30, 33, 35–6, 39, 41–5, 47, 51–2, 54, 59, 72, 78–81, 117, 121, 130–1, 133–5
Cooper, H. 83
Corder, S. P. 7
critical thinking test 52, 60
Cuddy, C. L. 30, 57, 93, 142
cue-probability learning (CPL) task 30, 39, 44, 52, 60–1, 64
Curran, T. 127
Cushman, D. 7

Davids, K. 15, 22–3
Davis, J. H. 30, 32, 46
Davis, J. 8–9
de Larios, R. 9
Deffner, G. 15, 17, 18, 21–2, 56–7, 80, 149
Dellick, D. M. 30, 57, 93, 142
di Vesta, F. J. 24–6, 41, 46
Dickson, J. 47, 51, 61, 63
Dominowski, R. L. 24, 41, 46–8
Druhan, B. 31, 43–5, 56–7, 83, 141, 146
Dubin, R. 76
Durst, R. K. 6

Earthman, E. A. 6
effect sizes,
    calculation of 82–3
    Cohen's *d* (interpretation) 82–3
    combination of 84–6
    definition of 77–8
El Dinary, P. B. 8–9
El Mortaji, L. 9
Ellis, R. 2, 12, 14, 118
Enkvist, I. 8–9

Ericsson, K. A. 2, 3, 5, 13–16, 18, 24–5, 27, 32, 43, 46, 52, 54, 56, 59, 64, 70–1, 110, 114, 117, 119, 138
Evans, J. S. B. T. 43–4
Evans, S. W. 30, 57, 93, 142
Ewert, P. H. 5

Færch, C. 8–9
Farrington-Flint, L. 6
faulty network 17, 19, 60
Fehrenbach, C. R. 6
Félix-Brasdefer, J. 10
Fidler, E. J. 24, 39, 40–1, 46, 63
Folger, T. L. 6
Foote, R. 86
forest fire-fighting (simulation) 47, 51–2, 60–1, 63–4
Fowler, L. P. 5
Foxman, P. N. 30, 32, 46
Fraser, J. 9
Fresch, M. J. 7
Friedman, P. 6

Gagné, R. H. 5, 24–8, 32, 46
gambles 54–5, 57, 60
Garcia, G. E. 128
Gardner, R. C. 78
Gass, S. 1, 8, 14, 113, 116–7
Gavin, C. A. 7
geometrical puzzles 17–18, 21, 57, 60
Goo, J. 78, 80–3, 89
Gordon, C. J. 6
Green, A. J. F. 7
Greenwood, J. 6

Hafner, J. 24–6, 28, 41
Hagafors, R. 37, 39, 61
Hamp-Lyons, L. 15, 22–4, 56, 58, 80, 149
Harmon, J. M. 6
Harvey, D. J. 24, 31–3, 46
Hashim, F. 9, 128–9
Hatasa, Y. A. 9
Hayes, J. R. 9
Hedges, L. 83–4
Hehir, J. 9
Herwig, A. 9
Heydemann, M. 15–18
Hines, A. M. 5

homogeneity test, use and
   calculation of 85–6; *see also*
   Q test
Hoosain, R. 6
Hosenfeld, C. 8, 10
Huang, H.-T. 78, 82
Hughes, J. 6
Hyona, J. 6

Iberri-Shea, G. 78, 82, 89
insight problems 31, 37, 60
investment analysis 17, 19, 60

Jaaskelainen, R. 8–9
Jannausch, U. H. 9
Jeon, K. S. 10
Jimenez, R. T. 128
Johnson, E. J. 24, 54–7, 59, 62–3,
   80, 84, 149
Jones, L. A. 6
Jourdenais, R. 2, 14–15
Just, M. A. 24–6, 29, 41, 46, 62

Kaimi, T. 9
Karsenty, L. 6
Kasper, G. 8–10
Katona card problem 46–8, 50,
   60, 78
Katona,G. 1
Keck, C. M. 78, 82, 89
Kellerman, E. 10
Kern, R. G. 8–9
King, M. 6
King, W. L. 29, 30, 46
Kirby, K. 6
Klettke, W. 15, 17–19, 56–8, 96,
   101, 105, 141
Knoblich, G. 15, 21–2
Ko, M. H. 9
Kojima, K. 9
Kotler-Cope, S. 31, 34–5, 44–6,
   57, 61, 141
Krippendorf, K. 130
Kuylenstierna, J. 43, 53

Lado, B. 72, 75, 80, 87–8, 94, 103,
   109, 115–18, 120, 142
Lambert, J. F. 5
Lapkin, S. 1, 9
Lass, U. 15, 17–19, 56–8, 96, 101,
   105, 141

Lee Thompson, L. C. 9
Lee, D.-S. 9
Lee, S.-K. 78, 82
Lee, T. M. 6
Leow, R. P. 1, 2, 8, 11–13, 67–9,
   71, 73–4, 88, 92–3, 108, 113–14,
   117–18, 121, 124–5,139, 141,
   144, 147
Light, R. 76–7, 83
Liljegren, J. E. 43, 53
Lin, H.-J. 72, 75, 80, 87–8, 94,
   103, 109, 115–18, 120, 142
Liu, J. 10
logic problem 21–2, 60
Lomicka, L. 8
Long, M. 10
Lüer, G. 15, 17–19, 56–8, 96, 101,
   105, 141

MacGregor, D. 10
Mackey, A. 1, 8, 10, 14, 78, 80–3,
   86, 89, 113, 116–17
Maeng, U. 9
Marin, J. 9
Markee, N. 123–5
Marks, M. R. 5
Marsiglia, C. S. 6
Masgoret, A. M. 78
Mathews, R. C. 31, 43–6, 56–7,
   83, 141, 146
McDonough, K. 8, 10
McGeorge, P. 34, 46, 61
McGuire, K. L. 6
McLennan, J. 47, 51, 61, 63
Meister, C. 6
meta-analysis,
   characteristics of studies in
      86–90
   coding for studies in 81–2
   selection criteria for studies in
      80–1
   types of 78
metacognitive report, definition of
   13
metalinguistic (report) 13
Midanik, L. T. 5
Morgan-Short, K. 2, 67–9, 71,
   73–4, 108, 114, 117–8, 121,
   139, 141, 144
Mulhern, S.T. 6
Murphy, L. 9

Nabei, T. 8, 10
Naquin, P. J. 6
Nassaji, H. 8
Nevo, N. 8–9
Nisbett, R. E. 14
Nissen, M. 127
Nist, S. L. 6
non-metacognitive report, definition of 13
non-metalinguistic (report) 13
Norris, J. M. 78, 80–2
Norris, S.P. 7–9, 52–4
Nurminen, A.-M. 6

O'Neill, M. 1, 8, 12, 114, 126–8
Ohlsson, S. 24, 31, 36–7, 46
Olive, T. 81
Olshtain, E. 10
Omodei, M. M. 47, 51, 61, 63
Ortega, L. 78, 80–2

Parkes, S. 6
Passino, C. 6
Payne, J. W. 14
Pearson, P. D. 128
Perkins, K. 7
Perpiñán, S. 86
personal interaction (simulator) 34, 38, 59–61, 64
Philp, J. 8, 11
Pillemer, D. 76–7, 83
Piolat, A. 81
Poehner, M. 1
Polio, C. 1, 9–10, 68–9, 73–4, 141, 145–6
Pollard, P. 43–4
Poulisse, N. 10
Pressley, M. 8
Pritchard, R. 8
probabilistic inference task 43, 60

Q test, use and calculation of 85–6
Qi, D. 1, 9

ranking course preferences 36, 60
Raven's (Standard Progressive) Matrices 16–18, 26, 29, 54–5, 57, 60–2, 64
reactivity, definition of 13–17
reactivity studies,
    in SLA 67–75

in non-SLA fields,
    comparing metacognitive and non-metacognitive reports 46–58
    comparing metacognitive reports and silent controls 25–46
    comparing non-metacognitive reports and silent controls 15–24
Rellinger, E. R. 24, 41, 46–8
retrospective (report) 1, 5, 8, 10–11, 13–15, 19, 31, 36–7, 41–3, 54, 117, 130
Rhenius, D. 15–18, 21, 56, 80, 149
Robertson, B. 6
Robinson, K.M. 5, 24, 39–40, 42–3, 46, 62
Robinson, M. 10
Robinson, P. 11
Ronowicz, E. 9
Rosa, E. 1, 8, 12, 114, 126–8
Rose, K. 10
Rosenshine, B. 6
Rosenthal, M. C. 80
Rosenthal, R. 76, 82
Rosman, A. J. 15, 17, 19
Rossomondo, A. E. 70, 75, 88, 92, 118, 141, 145
Rott, S. 9
Ruhlender, P. 15, 17–19, 56–8, 96, 101, 105, 141
rule learning task 29, 60
Russell, J. 78
Russo, J. E. 24, 54–7, 59, 62–3, 80, 84, 149

Sachs, R. 1, 9, 68–9, 74, 83, 88, 98, 103, 105, 115, 118–19, 141–2, 145, 147
Sanz, C. 72, 75, 80, 87–8, 94, 103, 109, 115–18, 120, 142
Scardamalia, M. 7
Schatschneider, C. 30, 57, 93, 142
Schell, P. 24–6, 29, 41, 46, 62
Schmid, R. 86
Schmidt, R. 11–12, 127
Schooler, J. W. 24, 31, 36–7, 46
Seguinot, C. 9
Seifert Kessell, N. 6

Selinker, L. 7
Seng, G. H. 9, 128–9
sentence assembly 17, 56–7, 60
Sergenian, G. K. 15, 17, 19
Shlesinger, M. 9
Short, E. J. 30, 35, 46, 56–7, 83, 93, 100, 142, 144, 146
Shymansky, J. 83–4
Simon, H. A. 2, 3, 5, 13–16, 18, 24–5, 27, 32, 43, 46, 52, 54, 56, 59, 64, 70–1, 110, 114, 117, 119, 138
simulated soccer games 22–3, 60
single judgment task (GPA prediction) 40–1, 60, 63
Smagorinsky, P. 1
Smith, E. C. 5, 24–8, 32, 46
Soeda, E. 9
Spada, N. 78
Spadacini, G. 6
Stafford, C. A. 72, 75, 80, 87–8, 94, 103, 109, 115–18, 120, 142
Stanley, W. B. 31, 34–5, 44–6, 57, 61, 141
statistics problems 41, 60
Stayton, S. 5, 24–5, 29, 41, 47, 50, 51
Steinberg, I. 128
Stencil Design Test 28
Stephens, D. L. 24, 54–7, 59, 62–3, 80, 84, 149
stimulated recall 1, 10–11, 14, 117
Stinessen, L. 31, 33–4
Storey, P. 7
Stratman, J. F. 15, 22–4, 56, 58, 80, 149
subtraction 40, 42, 60, 62, 64
sugar production (simulator) 34, 59–61, 64
Suh, B. R. 69, 74, 88, 118, 142, 145, 147
Swain, M. 1, 2, 8, 10, 137
Swift, C. 5, 24–5, 29, 41, 47, 50, 51
syllogistic reasoning 43–4, 60

Taguchi, N. 10
Tarr, D. B. 30, 32, 46
Taveggia, T. 76
temperature regulation (simulation) 21–2, 60

think-alouds,
  coding 126–36
  instructions for 113–16
  inter-coder reliability and,
    simple percentage agreement method 136
    Cohen's kappa method 136
  recording 120
  transcribing 123–5
  use in non-language fields 5–6
  use in L1 research 6–7
  use in L2 research 7–12
  warm-up tasks for 117
Thomas, M. 82, 89
Tomlin, R. S. 11
Tower of Hanoi 25–8, 32–3, 46, 50, 59–60, 62, 64, 78
Tracy-Ventura, N. 78, 82, 89
Type 1 (verbalization) 14, 56
Type 2 and 3 (verbalization) 14, 56

Upton, T. A. 9
Uzawa, K. 9

Valenti, C. 6
valuation 20–1, 60
veridicality 13–14, 54
Villa, V. 11
Vygotsky, L. 2, 137

Wade, S. E. 6
Walczyk, J. 6
Walters, F. S. 1
Wa-Mbaleka, S. 78, 82, 89
Wang, H. 7
Wang, J. 73, 75, 87–8, 92–4, 106, 109, 118, 141, 146
Wang, W. 9
Warren, J. 8
Wason's selection task 30, 36, 60
Wdowczyk-Szulc, J. 6
Weber, R. P. 130
Wen, Q. 9
Wheaton, A. 7
Wijgh, I. F. 7
Wilder, L. 24, 31–3, 46,
Wilhelm, J. 6
Williams, A. M. 15, 22–3
Wilson, T. D. 14, 31, 36–7, 46

Witte, S. P. 81
Wood, C. 6
Woodfield, H. 130–1, 133–5
Woodworth, G. 83–4
word puzzles 17–18, 21, 57, 60
Wright, W. F. 37

Yamashita, J. 8–9

Yang, Y.-F. 8
Yewchuk, C. R. 6
Yoshida, M. 71, 75, 88, 118, 142, 145

Zambarbieri, D. 86
Zellermayer, M. 6
Zutell, J. B. 7